cot

This
sho
by
tele
on

....
....
....
....
....
....
....
....
....
....
....
....

L.28

BIG SHOT

BIG SHOT

An autobiography

Geoff Capes

with Neil Wilson

Stanley Paul
London Melbourne Sydney Auckland Johannesburg

Stanley Paul & Co. Ltd

An imprint of the Hutchinson Publishing Group

3 Fitzroy Square, London W1P 6JD

Hutchinson Group (Australia) Pty Ltd
30–32 Cremorne Street, Richmond South, Victoria 3121
PO Box 151, Broadway, New South Wales 2007

Hutchinson Group (NZ) Ltd
32–34 View Road, PO Box 40-086, Glenfield, Auckland 10

Hutchinson Group (SA) Pty Ltd
PO Box 337, Bergvlei 2012, South Africa

First published 1981
© Geoff Capes 1981

Set in Baskerville by
A-Line Services, Saffron Walden, Essex

Printed in Great Britain by The Anchor Press Ltd
and bound by Wm Brendon and Son Ltd,
both of Tiptree, Essex

British Library Cataloguing in Publication Data
Capes, Geoff
  Big Shot
  1. Capes, Geoff
  2. Shot putting
  3. Track and field athletes – Great Britain –
  Biography
  I. Title
  796. 4'35'0924   GV1094

ISBN 0 09 144970 7

Copyright photographs are acknowledged as follows: *Sunday Times*; Tim Pike; Tony Duffy/All-
Sport; *Daily Mail*; Eamonn McCabe; *Daily Mirror*.
Cartoon by courtesy of the *Daily Mail*; action
photographs of Geoff Capes by courtesy of Howard Payne.

Contents

Foreword
by Neil Wilson

The idea for this book was first mentioned to me, as I recall, during an interview Geoff gave me for a magazine article as far back as 1973; it had been in Geoff's own mind as long as he had been an international athlete.

It does not set out to be a precise chronological account of an athlete's career, but is rather the opportunity Geoff has always sought to have his say, to answer back and put the record straight.

The book is based on a pot-pourri of scribbled thoughts and memories which Geoff has accumulated on his way. To that simple frame have been added thousands of words he poured onto tapes in the final months before the 1980 Olympics, in quiet moments everywhere from Haringey to Holbeach, Osterley to Oslo.

All the words in normal type are Geoff's own, as edited by me. His idiom has been closely retained throughout; where that entails mixing metric with imperial measurements, the purist must accept that this was how an athlete of his generation thought about his sport. The words in italic type are my comments.

Both of us owe thanks to those who freshened memories: to the Huggins family, Tommy Clay, and especially to Stuart Storey and to Geoff's family. But, most of all, this book owes its existence to the sport's administration – to those officials who could never accept that athletes have minds of their own and wish to speak them.

The great irony may yet be that Geoff Capes, already since this book was written elected chairman of the International Athletes Club and a member of the board of the Sports Aid Foundation's Eastern Region, will prove himself an abler administrator than any of them.

6

1

Unhappy Endings

Stuart Storey came down from his commentary position high in the Lenin Stadium like a man who had seen but not believed. He had finished a great day's work, a commentary on the finest Olympic pole-vault competition of all time, a classic duel between Poles and French and a Russian which had culminated in a world record.

But he could not bring himself to talk of it. Out of the corner of his eye, towards the other end of the stadium, he had seen a man to whom he had given nearly half his life, a man whom he had helped develop a technique for putting a shot better than any thrower of his generation, throw away an Olympic medal.

Time would ease the pain. In another hour he would reason with his memory and feel only sorrow. But, for those first few moments, in that dark, confined corridor beneath the stadium terraces, there was only anger, bitterness and recrimination.

The producer back in the London studios had asked whether he would like to do an interview with his man, Geoff Capes, the thrower he had steered since his schooldays in Lincolnshire. He could not face it. The two men were not to meet for another twenty-four hours.

'What would I say to him? Tell me that. Bad luck? Luck didn't enter into it. He performed like a wet cabbage.'

On another day, he might regret his anger, but now no insult, no criticism could be contained. His fury exploded from deep down, fuelled by the frustration of four years of feeling that what had happened in Montreal would be redeemed in Moscow.

It was not to be. Geoff Capes had finished fifth in his final competition in a major international championship. He had thrown 20.50 metres with his first throw to lie second, then slowly fallen back as he threw the worst series of his season, and allowed others to pass him.

'He knew what to do. We talked about it enough. He even did it right in the warm-up. And when he threw that first 20.50 I thought, "That's right, lad, you've taken the pressure off. Now go back and win it."

'What did he do? Nothing, absolutely nothing. His technique fell apart. He forgot everything, everything we had talked about, everything we knew could go wrong and what to do if it did. He let himself down, he let me down, he let down everybody who had ever given him anything.

'It was total lack of discipline. It was Montreal all over again. I couldn't believe my eyes. Four years we had spent finding out what went wrong there and how to overcome it. And it all happens again.

'Sorry? No, I'm not sorry. I'm just bloody angry. I've never felt such aggravation. It's all over and it's been just a bloody waste of time. Four years and thousands of hours and for what? How do I tell my wife that she's cooked all those meals for him for fifth place, that that's what I've devoted all my spare time to all these years? How does he tell his own poor wife?'

A drink cooled him. 'I'd have settled for a bronze for him, just something to take away from this place. It wasn't much to ask. He was capable of it. Oh God, Geoffrey, why the hell did you have to pick today to blow it!'

Am I a failure? Is fifth place in the Olympic Games a failure? Is the best place by a British shot putter at the Olympics since 1908 failure? Do sixty-seven international appearances for your country, more points and more wins for your country than any other athlete, add up to failure? I don't feel like a failure. I feel like a guy who on the day was the fifth best in the world, fifth best in the Olympic Games.

Of course I wanted to win a medal. I'd have loved to have taken away something from Moscow after all those years as an international athlete, after three Olympic

Games. Nobody wanted that more than I did, not Stuart, not my family, nobody.

There is nobody to blame. Just blame the time, the place and the hour. It wasn't my time. Now I'll never have another chance but don't tell me others are angry. It would have been my medal, and it is me who is going to miss it most.

But I'm not a failure. If I were, the Olympics would be full of hundreds of failures – thousands in every sport if you count those who never even qualified for them – who have never been the best in their country, never won anything. Athletics would be full of failures.

Look at the fine throwers who finished behind me: the East German Jacobi, the Yugoslav Milic, the Icelander Halldorsson – all great throwers. Look at Udo Beyer, the defending Olympic champion, struggling here for a bronze medal, a metre down on what he had done. Are they failures?

Every thrower in that competition had thrown 20.50 or more. And many were doing only about 19 metres here. You can't know what it is like throwing in the Olympic Games. It destroys you.

Look at Ruth Fuchs, ex-world javelin record holder and the Olympic champion. She was eighth in Moscow. What about Ferenc Paragi, the Hungarian who set a world record this year with the javelin? He was tenth – didn't even make the final cut. And what about Faina Melnik, the greatest discus thrower of them all? Is it eleven world records she's broken? Yet she was only fourth in Montreal and in Moscow she did not even qualify for the final.

All of them are experienced hands but all were unable to produce it on the day. I went out there and did everything I had been taught. I felt good. The first throw was exactly as I had hoped. I kept warm, I put my tracksuit on between throws, I warmed up at the right moments. But it wasn't there.

It wasn't like Montreal. There my mind froze. I couldn't do what I knew I should be doing. I couldn't think. In Moscow it was physical; suddenly there was nothing there, nothing came out. I wanted to do it desperately but my body refused.

Perhaps I had asked too much of my body in the past, and getting me through to the final was all it had left to give. I had to have two pain-killing injections in my lumbar region before the qualifying competition because of the pain there and I was stiff all over after it.

Perhaps the real turning point was when I had a recurrence of my old back trouble three or four weeks before the Games. I was lying watching the television in my own lounge. When I came to get up, I could not move. It was so bad that I had to drag myself up the stairs to bed on my elbows.

That week I rested it, had physiotherapy and swam every day; I had been advised that swimming was good medicine. Just six days later I kept a promise to compete in the Talbot Games at Crystal Palace. I spent that Friday afternoon in bed at the Queen's Hotel, eased myself out and down to the stadium, and off a shortened technique threw almost 21 metres. But I had to pull out of competition in Norway and Sweden the following week, and that seriously affected my Olympic preparations.

My back had just had enough. It is a right mess anyway, and has been for years – discs, vertebrae, all shot to pieces, no lubricant left between them after the thousands of hours of lifting and throwing. I guess that is why my legs were so dead. All the power, all the whip from the lower back, was gone.

I know I have to stop now and leave it to the younger throwers. There isn't anybody yet to move into my place in Britain but I cannot carry on holding the fort. Too many athletes have gone on too long with injuries and ended up on walking sticks. It's not worth it.

It would have been nice to finish with a medal – nice for me, my wife, my kids, my parents, my coach. But it wasn't to be. I was 'hot' a month too soon. So was Beyer. We were 'on' then. On the big day we were a metre down. And that is what the Olympics is all about; it is not about who is the best ever, or even the best of the year, but who is best on an appointed day. And on that day, it can be only one guy, and it wasn't me. It won't ever be me.

I can take that. What hurts is that when it mattered I didn't fulfil my potential. I saw the Cuban girl, Sarria, crying because she had not reached the final in the shot. What hurts is knowing that you haven't fulfilled yourself.

And it's you, above all, who knows that.

You don't need coaches, managers or the media to tell you that; you are your own best critic. I *know* I am not useless just because I didn't win, but what I do know hurts.

At least I made the final. I can't change the result and I have to be satisfied with it and live with it. Others can say all they like; if they haven't been out there in similar situations, they won't, in any case, know how it feels. Those of us who have, are going to spend the rest of our lives wondering what might have been. . . .

2

In the Beginning

Holbeach is a small thirteenth-century market town – one of those communities which cling to an existence on the flat Fens of England, not much more than a main street off a road cutting through the dykes and drainage ditches which save this part of rural England from the sea.

It has a larger population today and its size has increased but, when Geoffrey Lewis Capes was born there on 23 August 1949, he was one of fewer than seven thousand inhabitants, Most worked the land, and still do today, and those not actually bending their backs in the potato and cabbage fields and the apple orchards were servicing those who did.

It is a hard, physical life and in winter, when the area is swept by the winds off the North Sea that have not let up since they left the Urals, it is an inhospitable place – a land so flat that every perspective is two-thirds sky.

Geoff, the sixth child of Eileen Capes and her first by her third marriage, to Bill Capes, was probably no more mischievous than the average lad of his generation but he was more conspicuous. He was big, like all his brothers, and attracted trouble like a light attracts moths.

The family had its critics. Notorious would be too strong a word in this quiet rural environment to describe their reputation, but it would be fair to say that the family's standards were not those of the average villager, and Geoff himself was not best known for his good works.

Tommy Clay, a local schoolteacher and athletics official who encouraged Geoff's athletics career in its earliest days, remembers him as 'something of a bully'. Neville Huggins, who was head boy at the George Farmer School, Holbeach's secondary modern, when Geoff was a new boy there, says he was the 'scourge' of his prefectorial year. 'His name was on every page of my bad book that year,' he says.

Years later, when Neville's father Henry, a local haulier and coal merchant, employed Geoff as an assistant coalman, Neville's first reaction of hearing the news was: 'Oh, bloody hell, not him!' But they became friends, worked well together and the Huggins's bungalow always has a welcome for him today.

There are others in Holbeach who will rub their jaws with less fond memories of his youth, and he has critics there to this day. Dick Kent Walsey, local deputy headmaster at the time, was even heard to say when Capes first showed athletic ability, 'If that boy ever represents England, I'll eat my hat.'

There were nine in the family. My father was my mother's third husband. The elder two were Braithwaites, the middle four Cannons and I was the first of three Capes. Until I was eleven we all lived together in three converted cottages in Back Lane – all two up two down, which meant we had three kitchens, three front rooms and six bedrooms. And, when we sat down to meals together, we needed all that room.

My father was a ganger. He offered his services to local farmers. It was a manual life – anything from potato and strawberry picking to flower pulling and simple haulage. When there was work around, the money was good enough, but in winter times were tough.

We had our own bit of land, and that meant everybody had to help on it. None of the family is small. Dad was the shortest but the boys were all more than six feet tall, and my mother and my sister Christine were both nearly six feet. And working on the land made us tough, too. But it was not an easy job keeping so many of us fed and clothed, and there were times when we had to go without, or had to wear clothes other families could have afforded to throw away.

I guess the Capes were not your average, run-of-the-mill family. We were a bit apart from the rest, we didn't have the best clothes and, most important, we were happy to stand up for ourselves. So was our mother. My elder brothers established something of a reputation at the local primary school; I think I improved on it.

I had this big chip on my shoulder because I didn't have all that the others had. I was always trying to prove myself as good as them in other ways. I had to be best. There wasn't much chance of that at school work. I wasn't thick but I preferred sport and more practical subjects. But I was the strongest. I was always the strongest. It has never been any other way. That way I could prove myself, impress, stand out from the pack.

The first fight I had with a teacher was when I was eight. He told a girl, a real teacher's pet, to put the name of anybody misbehaving in his absence on the black-board. When he came back, there was my name, top of the list. 'Right, Capes,' he said, 'out you come.' When I didn't move, he grabbed me from my seat. I hit him with it. That was a fight I lost. There weren't many.

I was always being chastised for something I had done. It was constant suppression. I felt it at home being the only boy among the four youngest. But it was worse at school. Soon I couldn't tolerate authority in any shape – teachers or prefects.

My mother was strict enough with me. She had to be, with so many children. I used to get a broom or a poker across my backside when I had been in trouble. At least, I did until the day I bent the poker. She knew then it was too late to change me.

But she always stood by us. One day the art master twisted my ear so hard he tore it, and made it bleed. I hated him. Mum really sorted him out. She went to the school and laid him out.

On another occasion, when I was on my way home from school – a typical eight-year-old schoolboy with satchel and cap on, running home as fast as I could – I bumped into a man and knocked the shopping from his hand. He thumped hell out of me, cut my lip and made my nose bleed.

When I got home, my mum went wild. She gave me a beating for getting into a fight and then took me out to find the bloke. She collared him off a bus and – *wham!* She laid him out too. She was 18 stone in her prime and wouldn't shy from anything.

There was a gang of us. My best mate was Geoff Smith, 'Smithy' to all of us. He was smaller than I was, and he had to wear irons in those days because of hip trouble. I used to carry him to school piggy-back style. We were inseparable, and I was his minder. But there were others – Vellum, McCall, Oliver, Ingall, and Halstead. When we moved up to the George Farm Secondary School, the head, Joe Fathers, lined us up. He had heard of our reputation. 'Right-o, I've four years to make or break you. What's it going to be?'

I wasn't the best loved boy at any school. The only time I was important to them was when I was playing sport. I had my uses then, and I always had a friendly relationship with the PE masters.

But, elsewhere, I lived up to my bad name. Even at home I was something of a black sheep among the girls. I remember going to the shops for my dad's Woodbines and nicking a bar of chocolate off the counter. He'd give me 9*d*. (4p) pocket money to go to the pictures each week but that left nothing for sweets.

Back home, dad said the change was 6*d*. short and sent me back to the shop. 'Hey, mister, you've given me sixpence short,' I said, but he was on to me.

'What about the chocolate, son?'

I ended up with a hiding and two days confined to my bedroom to learn that lesson.

Even my older brothers started chastising me. One once thumped me and knocked a tooth out. I still have the gap. He went into the Merchant Navy. It was probably to escape from me. The others went into the police force, and obviously they could not afford a younger brother who was trouble.

But I was having problems learning to live with my size. I was bigger and stronger than anybody of my own age and, when you're like that, other kids, particularly the older ones, tend to pick on you, just to prove themselves.

The trouble with Holbeach was that there was nothing to do. A dance on Fridays, cinema and football were the only alternatives to fighting. It was a bit like a cowboy town – too much physical strength around looking for an outlet. Kids would come from Long Sutton, Wisbech and Spalding to pick fights and, as I was the biggest guy around, it was me they were looking for and me the other lads pushed forward.

One evening, two boys from Spalding came into our youth club, pulled the plug out of the record player, shouted for me and told me to get out of town. Imagine it – in your village! Another time we tied some rivals from another village to the traffic lights in the main street.

I was good at sport and I was good at scrapping, and the two even occasionally mixed. I was banned from playing for Tommy Clay's youth football team for a year after thumping a referee. He was the father of the kid marking me. Each time I went into a tackle he blew against me. Finally he gave me a warning. After the match, he came looking for me, so I bopped him. I was reported and banned.

I was the village hard case, I suppose. I'd fight anyone and enjoy it. I was good at it. I'd knock somebody down as soon as look at them if they wanted trouble. People think only cities have hard cases, that you have to be an East Ender or a Glaswegian to be a toughie. City lads may be in a class of their own for nastiness, but for strength they are strictly Second Division.

When I was seventeen and courting Gillian, who was to become my wife, the wheel dropped off my old former post office van. I didn't have a jack so I held it up with my left hand while I put the wheel back with my right. When you are that strong, not many kids can beat you at anything.

There were many big kids around the Fens, and still

16

are. It would make a great recruiting area for young throwers and lifters. There was so much fighting; the youth club leader often made us put on gloves and settle it properly, fair and square. That way nobody was really hurt but you learnt how to look after yourselves.

Trouble pursued me everywhere. When I was chosen to represent Lincolnshire in the All-England Athletic Championships as a fourteen-year-old, I warmed up by hitting another kid during a house soccer match. The PE master told me I wouldn't be allowed to go to the championships because of it. But he had a soft spot for me – the only teacher who ever did – and he later changed his mind.

Even when I won the AAA indoor junior title at Cosford with my first throw of more than 50 feet, I came home to a punch-up. The trip from the Midlands involved train and bus and it was evening before I arrived in Holbeach. But at the bus station there was Smithy with a warning that there was a boy in town looking for me. That was that boy's first mistake; his second was to hit me.

I met him by a paper shop, across the road from Pledger's, the local cycle dealer. I didn't hit him, I just threw him and he flew across the road and through the shop window. Then I dusted him down, marched him to the police station and made him claim it was an accident and offer to pay for the damage. Another time when I was set on by two kids down by the church, I threw both of them over the church wall.

We had this gang called the Eagles. There must have been three hundred kids involved in it and, while most of what we did was good-natured fun, it had its bad moments.

A lot of those kids ended up in trouble with the police, and one or two ended up 'inside'. The way I was heading suggested it would happen to me too. Sport was the only thing I had to hang on to in my life, and my folks weren't interested in that. The first time either of them came to watch me compete was when I promoted my own international meeting in Holbeach. That was in 1977. That was how interested they were in me.

Fortunately, there was Stuart Storey. He was nearly seven years older than I, and something of a local hero. I used to run after him a bit. 'There's your spikes, Stuart; here's your tracksuit, Stuart.' Just hero worship stuff really – I wanted to be noticed.

Stuart Storey had noticed him all right. The potential talent of Capes was obvious. So were the potential problems. Finally, Storey took him on one side, told him he was mixing with the wrong crowd and that it would end in trouble with the police, and quoted him the example of a well-known 400 metres hurdler whose career had been prematurely ended in that way. 'I told him to put his aggression into his shot putting,' says Storey.

It was a timely warning. On a subsequent expedition, the Holbeach gang were caught shop-lifting in Spalding. Capes was not with them that day because of Storey's warning, but it was a salutary lesson for him.

It was not the end of Capes's career as a young tearaway. Storey had to lecture him again, this time on tolerance. 'He couldn't tolerate anybody or anything, and I gave him a full hour on the subject,' recalls Storey.

A week later, in the Windmill Cafe in Whaplode, Capes was dug in the back by a man carrying a stick. 'I remembered what you said,' he told Stuart later. 'I turned the other cheek. But he hit it with a bottle.'

Capes could claim one point in his favour. He had hit the poor man only once. 'When the ambulance man arrived, he kept looking about. Said it was for the railway line 'cause someone has been hit by a train.'

'His strength was enormous, and what people did not realize was how fast he was. He never asked questions first. He just didn't have the tolerance for that sort of approach. There's a lot of his critics still in Holbeach. He wasn't well liked outside his own group – too much of a villain for the average taste,' says Storey. 'Fortunately, his mates' being nicked was the turning point. He put all his energy into shot putting after that.'

I put all my hate into those 16 pound balls. If an opponent wanted aggro, I'd vent my feelings on the shot. If an opponent taunted me, called me a big hairy ape – as more than one has – instead of landing one on him, I'd use the feeling in the next throw. It was like coal to the fire. Then, *bang* – you get your own back in the right way. Hit a person with the same explosiveness and his head would not be on his shoulders for very long. Shot putting and Stuart taught me to put my wildness to better use. Funny, isn't it? If I'd been a normal, quiet and respectable lad, I'd never have become one of the world's best shot putters.

Stuart was at Loughborough College and already an international athlete. I was only fifteen but he was all I had ever needed. Somebody to take an interest in me – I made the choice to dedicate myself to becoming a champion and I haven't had a punch-up – for the fun of it – since that day. Athletics became everything to me. Within a year of finishing second to last in the All-England Schools Championship, I improved 15 feet to become the best youth in Britain. I was on my way.

3

Picking up the Basics

There are a thousand Tommy Clays in Britain. Everywhere there are clubs and societies, there are men like him — the lifeblood of sport.

You rarely read of them because they do not aspire to power and position outside their own districts, content usually to keep close to their roots and nurture them. And, with those sort of men around, clubs prosper.

Tommy Clay, a local schoolteacher, formed Holbeach Athletic Club in May 1949, just three months before Geoff Capes was born. Its only track was the grass of the local Carter's Park and, even today, thirty years later, the club has to travel to Spalding to run on anything better.

But the club's establishment and development was crucial to the Capes story. Clay himself says, 'Geoff was lucky in one important way. He was born into a time and a place in which the environment was right for athletics.'

Had he been born a few miles further south in St Ives, he might have ended up in Andy Smith's stable as a boxer, like local boy, Joe Bugner. But Holbeach was a place for throwers and lifters.

'Ten years before Geoff appeared on the scene, there was no local athletics except for a few handicap 100 yard events at local horse and cycle shows,' says Clay. 'But people here don't move like sprinters. Nothing happens fast. We're not competitive in the way urban people are. Life's a bit slower, a bit of plod. It's a place for marathon runners really but, because of the manual labour, it's even more a place for strong men and throwers.'

Clay encouraged field events, and soon a group grew up around a local lad, Bruce McEwan, who now runs his own asphalt company and is the inspiration behind Holbeach's first squash

club. McEwan, one of many who were to employ Capes briefly,
ranked among the top ten shot putters in Britain in the mid-1960s
and became a useful decathlete.

Clay helped put down a rough throwing circle in Carter's Park,
encouraged the national coaches to visit and acted as chauffeur for
training trips to RAF Feltwell in Norfolk. 'McEwan and another
club member, John Watts, taught Geoff the rudiments of throw-
ing, and it's to Stuart Storey's credit that he sorted him out. But
you have to give Geoff some of the credit – he was always big,
strong and quick.'

The first time I ran it was for money. I didn't know, of
course. That wasn't the incentive. I was only six. They
had to put me in the under-nines race because I was too
tall for the under-sevens, and I won it wearing wellington
boots. The prize was a book token worth 7s. 6d. (37½p).
This was a fair amount of money twenty-five years ago
and, as the family was a bit skint as always, we changed
it for cash.

That was also the first time I remember seeing Stuart
Storey. It was the annual Holbeach sports day in Carter's Park in the first week of August. He must have been
about thirteen, and it was a long time before we were to
become close, but he must have made some sort of
impression on me for the memory to have stuck.

Sport began for me at school. I was an all-rounder. I
played basketball and football and did gymnastics. I
played soccer for Lincolnshire Schools, basketball for
Holland County and represented my school in just about
everything. But first and foremost I was an athlete; I was
tall and slim, and could run. Most of all I loved cross
country – a bit of a Brendan Foster really – and I fancied
myself a bit over 800 metres. It was that event which won
me my first selection for my secondary school, George
Farmer's, when I was eleven. We were to compete
against Donnington School.

Donnington had a boy we knew as Tank. He could
throw a bit. Our school did not have a thrower, and I

happened to be the biggest boy available. So in I went, threw the 6 pound shot 36 feet 8 inches and that was it. Capes was the school shot putter. It was a job for life, and not one I especially wanted at the time.

As it happened, that day I also won the 800 metres, the discus and the javelin, ran in both relays and helped the school to victory, but from then on I was a shot putter. Fortunately, the one teacher I had taken a liking to, the PE master Gary Cooke, was keen on athletics. So I had every encouragement from him. My best achievements were: high jump – 5 feet 8 inches; triple jump – 42 feet; long jump – 18 feet 10 inches; 100 yards – 10.5 seconds; and 1 mile – 4 minutes 48 seconds. Not a bad collection that.

Thoughts of entering decathlon events were not yet in my mind, but eventually I did compete in one such competition at Peterborough. This was much later, when I was just seventeen, in October 1966, and I finished second, using junior implements, with a score of 5565. A year later, I scored 3101 to win a pentathlon at Lincoln. But in that first year at secondary school I was better suited to running than throwing. I was tall but not big; the truth is I was a bag of bones. I was proud of my strength and always trying to prove it but I wasn't too happy with how I looked. My appearance was brought home to me one day in a sweet shop, when a woman took a dislike to my not wearing a shirt. 'You ought to be ashamed of yourself, looking like that,' she said. 'You look like a Belsen victim.'

I put my shirt back on and crept away. For somebody whose only heroes were muscle men – Steve Reeves, Reg Parks, Tarzan – it was the worst insult imaginable. I determined to do something.

Next door to my home was a scrap dealer's yard. I'd often run loose in it but my next visit after this incident had a purpose. I was looking for a metal bar to use for weightlifting. And I found it. It must have weighed 100 pounds. Every night I would lie in bed trying to push it off my chest.

It was about that time that a group of us formed the Weightlifting Club of Holbeach. Two local farmers bought us some weights, and we used the stage of our youth club as a base. A piano at one end was the weights' trestle. It couldn't last – we kept dropping the weights through the stage!

Finally we transferred to the back room of the Chequers pub, and then later, when the local council was getting rid of some wartime pre-fab houses, we bought one to convert into a proper clubhouse. It is still there today, prospering.

Throwing was almost a sideline. I was keener on weightlifting. My record for a bench press at the club was 575 pounds and, when I was eighteen, I lifted 535 pounds in a competition. I lifted more than 600 pounds in a dead lift when I was still a junior, and won the North-east Midlands junior strength set and Olympic set titles two years running. The first time, at Louth, the national coach, John Lear, had to show me how to perform the snatch technique just before the contest started. I was not so hot on technique but I had all the necessary strength and aggression.

My first major athletics appearance was in the All-England Schools Championships at Hendon in 1964. Joe Bugner, who was to become British heavyweight boxing champion, won the discus that year. I was second to last in the shot. I would have been last with my throw of 42 feet 6 inches but the guy behind me made three fouls!

It goes to show that you cannot write kids off too soon. Mike Winch finished ahead of me that day but never beat me again. I just wonder what happened to the other guys in that competition. They had something I didn't have on that day. Perhaps it was only their superior footwear. The best shoes I had was a pair of Woolworth plimsolls which were next to useless for shot putting.

I did not get another chance in the England Schools. At the end of that summer term I was only a month short of my fifteenth birthday, so I didn't bother to go back again. I was getting nowhere with school work. I joined my dad on the gangs doing manual labour around the Fens, straw cutting, picking 'taters – anything physical.

I just needed more training. All the time, I was thinking about getting bigger and stronger, and looking better. Everything was a training exercise. I wouldn't just lift a bag of potatoes. I would 'clean' it and do ten presses with it before putting it on the stack.

When I tried, I could load a lorry faster than five men. I once loaded 20 tons of potatoes on a cart in twenty minutes to show it could be done. But I didn't hold jobs long. I drifted. Athletics was my whole life. I was sacked from one job as a delivery man for a mineral water company; I claimed I was sick and competed in London when I should have been making a delivery to a Saturday show. The boss caught me out. He saw me on television!

Geoff did have one more chance to mix with schoolchildren. Storey, now a teacher at Dr Challoner's Grammar School in Amersham in Buckinghamshire, arranged with his head of department, Dr Alan Lauder, to co-opt him for the school athletics team's summer tour of Germany. Challoner's was not Geoff's usual scene. It was a true grammar school, high in academic standards and full of children of middle-class families from the London stockbroker belt. But Geoff mixed well.

The problem was persuading the opposition that he was only a schoolboy. Here was this giant of fifteen years, then about 6 feet 3 inches tall, who just did not fit the image of Challoner's. Storey recalls the problem that was caused by the shot putt judges in Germany, who would insist on standing only 15 metres from the circle. 'Geoff was having to use a 14 pound shot – as they do on the continent – 2 pounds more than an English junior shot, but I warned the officials what he would do,' says Storey. 'First time Geoff throws the thing right over their heads. You should have seen them scatter.'

Challoner's used Capes for several events. In the hammer he was less than successful. 'Geoff went further out of the circle than the hammer,' says Storey. But he was an outstanding success on the last leg of the relay in Coblenz, taking the school from fourth to first.

The other boys pressed him continually to prove his strength. In one beer garden, they had him lying on the floor lifting a bench with boys still sitting on it. But the social gulf was highlighted during a storm. 'The camp site was awash, the boys were awake, wet and cold and I couldn't sleep. But there was Geoff, sound asleep in my tent with a little river of water running an inch from his nose.

'These well-heeled kids could not believe that they had given up their lovely homes in England for this misery. But Geoff slept through it. He had slept rough so often that it took more than a spot of water to spoil his night!'

Athletics has changed dramatically since I began making my way up the ladder. In my teens there were no expenses provided to allow you to travel in any style to events. I hitchhiked to most places. Today you get kids demanding to know what transport is laid on. I had a sixteen-year-old in one of my AAA teams recently who wanted to know how he was going to get from north London to west London!

My mother and father never had a car and would not have been bothered to drive me about if they had had. When I won my first titles, the shot and discus at the Northern Youth Championships, it was Tommy Clay who drove three of us from the club to Hull. And we brought back four medals between us. But, more often than not, I had to make my own way – bus, train and usually a hitched lift. Holbeach was not the easiest place to get to without a car. When I competed at the AAA Junior Championships at Kirkby, near Liverpool, as a sixteen-year-old, public transport would only get me back as far as Peterborough. Late at night, I had to use £3 10*s.* (£3.50) – all I had on me – to take a taxi the rest of the way home.

My big heroes at the time were Tony Elvin and Cornelius Ellerbroek, two big lads from Norfolk who both trained at RAF Feltwell. Tommy often took us to Felt-well for training and occasionally for competition, and when I was sixteen I threw against Tony. I did 48 feet 4½ inches and he won with something over 52 feet. But he was impressed with me, and said so, and that was a memorable compliment, coming from the man ranked fourth that year in Britain behind Martyn Lucking, Mike Lindsay and Jeff Teale.

What I did not have was a good technique. That I had any at all was due to the help and advice of McEwan, Watts, Chad Edwards and Chopper Carey – lads in the club who were not that much older than me. Without them, I would never have made it as far as I did; in 1966 I was already ranked thirtieth in Britain when I was still only sixteen.

We were having problems at Carter's Park. The groundsman had begun to stop our throwing sessions because of the dents we were making in his grass. It is the same everywhere: throwers are not the favourite sports-men among the groundsmen of the world. I remember one poor chap at Scunthorpe accusing Tommy Clay of allowing his kids to drop shots all over his lovely turf after the groundsman had gone to the trouble of marking out a 50 foot fan. What he had not allowed for was me. I'd been putting the shot beyond his fan. He couldn't believe a kid so young could putt it so far.

I was working now with the Huggins family. Neville had been Lincolnshire 440 yard champion and had run in the English Schools Championships, so the family was interested in the sport. His father Henry offered me a job as an assistant coalman and odd-job man. It was physical work again but it was great for the training programme.

There were plenty of weights around the yard for weighing freight and coal. They became part of my weight-training equipment. I would sit down on the weighing machine with 4 stone (56 pounds) in each hand and tap the weights together above my head. I got in trouble at times for wasting good working time but Neville and I became great friends.

26

We once took a lorry load of potatoes to London together, unloaded it at midnight, slept in the cab of the Ford truck, and then loaded 612 boxes of apples for the return journey. You get to know people that way. I stayed with the Huggins for eighteen months until I went into the police.

Athletically, it all seemed to be working. Stuart had been coaching me, and suddenly it began to come together. I was strong, I was tall, and my ability was starting to show in the feet and inches I was throwing.

4

The Young Pretender

Anyone mistaking movement for action might have been deceived into believing that British shot putting was making progress in the sixties. In fact, it had all the frenetic fervour of a headless chicken, and as little future.

Arthur Rowe, the outstanding thrower of the previous decade, had retired in 1962 to pursue more mercenary goals on the Scottish Highland circuit. As his last testament to the sport, he left his event in Britain with a standard his successors found impossible to equal.

Rowe's 1961 British record of 19.56 metres (64 feet 2 inches) was to stand for twelve years and, worse, there was nobody approaching within a foot of it in the mid-sixties. Martyn Lucking, Mike Lindsay and Jeff Teale, who had all shared international duties with Rowe before his retirement, were still the best and, though powerful Welshman Alan Carter challenged briefly, they were all far short of Rowe's record.

The national coaches in the north, Denis Watts and Wilf Paish, came up with an idea. They would stage a contest for strong men to find a suitable successor to Rowe. Television took up the stunt, and invitations to compete in strength tests in Leeds in March 1967 were sent to the north's most likely lads.

They came in all shapes and sizes — wrestlers, strong-arm acts, ballroom bouncers, powerlifters and even bodyguards! Several were older than Rowe himself, and the oldest was more than thirty-five. But the youngest was Geoff Capes, 17½ stone and 6 feet 5¾ inches that day, according to Paish's records, and still five months short of his eighteenth birthday.

Paish knew of Capes. He had heard of him from Clay, noticed him when he visited Holbeach and once seen him run a 1500 metres steeplechase as a schoolboy. But his first close encounter was on that March morning when a startled caretaker at Carnegie College in Leeds rang Wilf to say they had a giant asleep on their snooker table who, when awoken, had claimed he had come to win 'the Rowe competition'. Paish, thinking quickly, invited the giant to breakfast at his house.

They had invited me but nobody had sent any fare money, so it meant hitching to Leeds. I set off the night before, and made it there with fifteen lifts. The last was a lorry driver, heading for Leeds market. He offered me a ride in exchange for help in unloading. From three in the morning, I spent an hour humping his load.

Afterwards, I wandered along to Carnegie, found an open window and settled down for a few hours' kip on a billiard table. You can imagine the surprise of the students and the caretaker when they found me at about six o'clock! And, after a night of hitching, unloading and sleeping on a billiard table, I wasn't feeling brilliant myself.

The tests were all for strength. They had this machine called a Dynometer, which was used to test for back and leg strength and grip strength in each hand. Some of the older men were massively strong. One did 2300 pounds with his legs, and broke the machine.

My only victory was in the vertical standing jump. I did 26½ inches. But I was second equal with 650 pounds in the back test, second on right-hand grip with 195 pounds and on left-hand grip with 185 pounds and, amazingly, nowhere with 1750 pounds on legs. But I won overall with 345.5 points, ahead of a kid a year or two older called Ian McTigue.

The prize was a book presented by the British champion before Rowe, John Savidge, but the best part of winning was an invitation to White City that year for the Britain versus United States match. There I was, seventeen years old, sitting between the great American Jay

Silvester and Britain's Jeff Teale watching the world record holder Randy Matson compete with Neil Steinhauer.

Mind you, the television company made a mess of getting me there. Wilf Paish got me into the stadium but I had to get myself to London. More hitching! But that day I knew that shot putting was for me. Weightlifting had been tempting but now this was it. I remember telling Matson just that. 'I'm national junior champion and one day I'm going to be as good as you.'

In fact today Matson still ranks one place higher than I do in the all-time world lists. His best of 21.78 metres, which he did in 1967, is just 10 centimetres better than my 1980 British record. He was a helluva thrower, the greatest ever for me.

What a year 1967 was for me! In July I won my first junior international vest against France at Portsmouth. Britain had a fair old team out there that day. Ian Stewart and Tony Simmons were running 3000 metres, Paul Dickenson was throwing the hammer, Mike Winch was throwing the discus and Ralph Banthorpe was one of our sprinters.

The French had a fine team, too. Looking back at the results, I see that the fifth place man in the pole vault that day was none other than Guy Drut, with 13 feet $1\frac{1}{2}$ inches. Less than ten years later he was Olympic high hurdles champion.

The match was a tremendous boost for me. I beat Patrick Chala, the European junior record holder. It was an under-twenty match, and I was still a month short of my eighteenth birthday, but I won with a throw of 52 feet $2\frac{1}{2}$ inches. There was more to come. In September at Solihull I threw 52 feet $9\frac{3}{4}$ inches to rank tenth for that year among British seniors.

Nothing, it seemed, could stop me. In 1968 I putted 56 feet $7\frac{3}{4}$ inches and won all the junior titles. That ranked me seventh, and in my nineteenth year, still a junior, I finally passed Mike Lindsay to take fourth place on the British rankings with 57 feet 4 inches. Only Teale, Bill

Tancred and John Watts were ahead of me now and I was national indoor and outdoor junior champion.

Everything was going well. Stuart had gone to Kentucky in America for further studies but he had put me in the capable hands of Les Mitchell, a coach in Peterborough. That year I had one more junior international, when I won the shot but finished fourth in the discus. More British age records fell to me and, on my home ground in Holbeach in July 1968, I set a British junior record of 16.80 metres (55 feet 1½ inches). It still stood in 1980, which shows how good I was as a teenager, or perhaps how desperate has been the lack of talent following me into the event since my young days.

My bible was a book by Arthur Rowe and the former national coach Geoff Dyson. Dyson had coached Rowe to thirteen British records, and I swore by every word they said. It was called *Champion in Revolt* and it contained all the technical hints that interested me. If Rowe said he ate 4 pounds of steak a day, Geoff Capes would eat 4 pounds of whatever meat he could lay his hands on. Taking up someone else's diet so literally is not something to be advised because every thrower is different, but his book was a tremendous motivating force for me.

I was not thinking too much about Rowe's record in those days. My mind was on lesser targets. Each year I would set one, and often as not have to re-set it before the year was out. I remember the terrible trouble I'd had beating 50 feet for the first time. Every throw seemed to be 49 something. Then I went to Cosford for the under-twenty championships and blasted out 54 feet.

My ambition now was to get into the British senior team, and become number one. Teale was the king, the British champion. The first part of the ambition was achieved in 1969. I was chosen to partner Teale in an international match against Czechoslovakia in Brno. The second part was to take three more seasons.

Brno was an experience, whichever way you look at it. The throwing group on the team was Teale, Bill and Peter Tancred and myself, and I can remember Teale saying to me, 'You've come a long way to lose, lad.' He was a great guy and soon became a good friend, but I was the young whippersnapper who was pushing for his place and he wasn't going to do me any favours. He wanted to make sure I understood that.

I did not do myself too many favours that day. I threw 55 feet 11½ inches, which was below my best and only good enough for fourth place. Teale was second, beaten by the Czech Jiri Skobla, the 1954 European champion. But worse was to follow. That evening the Czechs invited us to an official reception in a rural spot outside town.

I had not eaten since lunchtime, but before we came close to the food the hosts brought around trays of drinks. I wasn't a drinker – not exactly teetotal but too interested in sport to have bothered with boozing. Anyway, the other lads threw back a few, so I followed suit. There was wine galore and a colourless liquid which I discovered later to be slivovitch. Before the food arrived, accompanied by glasses of more booze, we were all feeling the effects – officials as much as athletes. Finally, of course, all hell broke loose.

There are a lot of stories which have grown up around that night. Arthur Gold, who is now president of the European Athletic Association, was then the team manager and is fond of reminding me of them. Some are pure fantasy but those which are true hardly bear remembering.

Certainly I lost control of myself. I was an eighteen-year-old unused to drink who had had far too much. The first casualty was one of those huge wine barrels, cut out at one side so that people could sit inside it. I pushed it on its side and rolled it down the road. That was just for starters. Then I punched a hole in a barrel – yes, actually punched. When it came to getting back in the coach for the ride to town, there were bodies everywhere.

Poor Arthur had had to cope with athletes lying in ditches and his newest recruit breaking the place up. There was only one thing for it – I had to be silenced. Arthur's problem was that I was 6 feet 5¾ inches. So Bill

Tancred was asked to oblige. First Teale had to get hold
of me. Jeff always reminds me of Desperate Dan in the
comics – block head, square chin, usually with stubble
on it. And he was strong. He held me firm. Bill, unfortunately, had had the odd drink himself. Back came his
arm, across came an enormous fist and . . . *crash* – Teale
took the punch on the side of the head. After that, I
remember nothing. The flight home next day is just a
blur. The team doctor said I had had alcoholic hysteria.

Whatever the cause, the result was my disappearance
from the team for the rest of that season. The official
reason was that there were better throwers and that I
was injury prone. Both were true. It was about then that
my back became really bad. But I've always assumed
that the officials were also using the opportunity to put
me in my place. My behaviour had been noted. Drink
was never a problem again for me, but from that moment
I would not be allowed to forget I was a troublemaker.

5

The Takeover Bid

At the age of thirteen, Capes fell 20 feet from a wall. He landed on his feet, and appeared to be none the worse for it. But he suffered injuries that were not then apparent but which were to affect him throughout his career. In Brno, seven years after the fall, he noticed them for the first time. His back ached, and there was stiffness and sometimes sharp pains near the base of the spine.

Had I been the junior champion of the Soviet Union or East Germany, I would have been whisked away to the top specialist immediately and put right. In Britain it took me six months to get near to a specialist.

Fortunately, when I did see a Dr Woodard in Wimpole Street in 1969, he was the best. He saw the problem immediately. The fall had jarred my spine, vertebrae had fused and the nerves had been trapped. For the last seven years I had developed on my right side but not on my left. I was lopsided.

That same day he manipulated my back into its correct position, and within six weeks I was training again without pain. The problem has never entirely left me. I need frequent physiotherapy, I must warm up well and I have lost count of the number of pain-killing injections I have needed in the back before competition.

Heavy weightlifting, particularly when I was still growing, obviously did not help the problem, but it was the fall which had started the rot. It will never improve

34

now, and it was in some measure responsible for my failure in Moscow in 1980.

After my visit to Dr Woodard, my back appeared cured, and I was training again, when a second blow struck. I had to have an operation for a hernia. This is a common weightlifters' problem and it was not a major tear in my stomach wall, but it meant more weeks out of action.

Fortunately it all happened in winter. When the Commonwealth Games trials came round the following summer, I was fit again – and good enough to finish second to Teale. I had made it. The dream had come true. I cannot remember a more fantastic moment than receiving my letter informing me I had been selected for England's team.

I knew by now that I was going to be the best in Britain. Teale was thirty already. He was very strong but he could not go on for ever. Lindsay was another powerful man, while Lucking had more finesse, but both were thirty-one. Beating them was no longer enough. I had not yet beaten Teale in competition but even that was only a matter of time. What mattered now was becoming the best Briton ever. That was the target and that meant beating my great hero, Arthur Rowe.

I had not met him until the Commonwealth Games in Edinburgh, as he had spent most of the previous eight years on the Highland Games circuit. In 1966 at Pitlochry he had even been awarded a prize for being the best of the Highland heavies. But, for me, he was still just a great shot putter, the greatest technician of his generation – utterly brilliant.

That day he did not live up to my boyhood dreams. I asked him if I might train with him. 'How much is it worth to you?' he said. I could not believe my ears. I still hope it was a lousy joke. It had been his own choice to turn professional. He might have regretted it then, knowing that, if he had not done so, he might have gone on to win Olympic titles, but nobody had forced him to make the decision.

I finished fourth in Edinburgh. Teale was second and the Canadian Steen won the gold medal. That was not my only experience at the Games. The other throwers drew me into one of their nights out. I thought at the time I was being initiated. I lost count of the number of pints we drank, and then off we went to a house of ill repute. I even lent one of them the money but I sat in the lounge, feeling very young and innocent. I still did not feel part of their world.

My determination to beat them all now was unbearable. Teale would keep repeating that catchphrase he used when he beat me: 'You've come a long way to lose, lad.' I wanted to ram it down his throat. He knew all the tricks, the gamesmanship, the professional niggling that the crowd doesn't see. There are four-letter words which translate into any language, and everyone has their own way of putting others off.

Mike Winch was vulnerable to noise. He went white if anybody spoke when he was throwing. It was easy enough to drop a shot or something when he was in the circle. Teale taunted me all the time. But when he beat me at the AAA Championship that August, 1970, it was for the last time. I did not have to wait long for my turn.

The breakthrough came in Britain's match against Poland in Warsaw on 12 September, just a few weeks after I had thrown only 17.04 metres (55 feet 11 inches) in Edinburgh. That's a left-handed standing putt to me today, and even then I knew I could do better. My big one came first: 17.72 metres (58 feet 2¾ inches). It was near enough a personal best. The Poles, Edmund Antczak and Tadeusz Sadza, were well ahead, but Teale was not doing well.

The next throw exploded from him. He was determined to beat me. *Crash!* It thudded into one of the metal pins the Poles were using as markers – and it was my pin he hit. They measured it right to my marker: 17.71 metres. Teale was furious. He stomped across the area and kicked the pin out of the ground. It did not matter. The measurements had been made. I was third, but that did not matter either. Teale was fourth. For the first time I had beaten him.

It was the end for Teale. It was not long after that he retired, going out in a blaze of publicity because he was alleged to have taken the drug anabolic steroid. But it was just the beginning for me. I have never since been beaten by another British thrower. What other British athlete can claim that record: unbeaten by any fellow countryman in hundreds of competitions over ten years? Good days and bad days, I have beaten every thrower from Britain who has challenged me, won seven AAA Championships – a record for any British shot putter – and six AAA Indoor Championships. That's what you call domination.

All that was left now was to wipe Arthur Rowe from the record book. He was going to be a hard man to beat. He may have retired nearly ten years earlier, but I looked up to him. When you respect a man for what he's done, it's hard to beat him. There's a mental block. There had been something similar with Teale. He was Rowe's successor. I respected him for that. But, once I had beaten him, even by only a centimetre, the block was gone. He was a dead man in my mind. Rowe was still there. The record was 64 feet 2 inches. It had been set in 1961. It was stamped indelibly on my mind.

That was the trouble. I could not stop thinking of it. A few days before beating Teale I had thrown a personal best of 17.73 metres at White City. That was my first 58 foot throw. A few months later, indoors at Cosford, came the first 59-footer, and my first 18 metre throw. At Shotley Gate, in May 1971, I was through the 60-foot barrier, and after that it was records all the way for that season.

Indoors and out, I improved my best eight times that year. I did it three times in June alone – at Loughborough, Edinburgh, where I threw my first over 61 feet, and Paris, where I combined my first 62-footer with my first over 19 metres.

That was a year, too, when I was thinking about following Joe Bugner's footsteps into boxing. I had been

working out for several months under boxing trainer
Paddy Lyons. I never did step into the ring for the real
thing. I was always reminded of the 1960 Olympic shot
champion Bill Neider, who did try to make money from
boxing. He was stopped in the first round of his only
contest. But the training was helping. It was making me
so much quicker. My reactions were improving, and I
was exploding across the circle more aggressively.

Seventy per cent of successful shot putting is a question of height, weight and strength, and the rest is speed,
technique and determination. That is why a naturally
tall person has the edge. Mike Winch has always had this
silly thing about being the best for his size. He's fast,
explosive and his technique is ideal for his height. But
what good is that if you are not big enough? They
don't give records or medals for size. Who is bigger,
smaller or has the best technique is irrelevant. It's how
far you throw the bloody thing that counts – feet and
inches, pure and simple. Teale kept saying, even after I
had long passed Rowe's records, wiped all of them off the
books, that Rowe was Britain's best ever. He argued that
I was inches bigger than Rowe, and that made Rowe's
record more impressive. That's nonsense. It's like saying
that Seb Coe's shorter than Steve Ovett, so his records
are better. I've thrown further from a standing putt than
Rowe ever did. That's how much better I am.

But even that is irrelevant. Rowe and I come from
different generations. All records improve. Shot is an
event where it is more reasonable than in other cases to
judge one generation against another. The shot weighs
the same and the techniques have remained largely
unchanged over the last twenty years. But is there any
point in these comparisons?

My greatest handicap has always been a mental one.
The major competitions seem to have produced a mental
block. I can meet the world's best throwers throughout
the year, and the challenge stimulates me. But, go into a
major Games, and I find something holding me back.
The European Championships in Helsinki in 1971 were

typical. On the last day of July in Holbeach I threw a personal best of 19.07 metres. Two weeks later in Helsinki I was a non-qualifier with 18.54 metres. One week after Helsinki I threw another personal best of 19.48 metres – my first 63 feet plus throw and just eight centimetres short of Rowe's record.

Perhaps I psyche myself out, talk myself out of winning. Perhaps I think negatively, respect the opposition too much. Rowe's record was beginning to do that to me. My first competition of 1972, the Olympic year, was at Newham, the Golden Wonder meeting. Presto, I'd equalled Rowe's record – not once, not twice, but three time in six throws. Think of it – three throws of exactly 19.56 metres, precisely, impossibly, identical. It was enough to make a man go off his head. It was as though Rowe had put up an invisible screen and my shot would never go through it. They could reach it but not break it.

There was only one thing for it. I had to find somebody who could work on my mind. I had heard that a Scottish coach, Bill Stevenson, who coached several of the Scottish girl throwers, had been working on hypnosis. It was worth the trip north. I met him in Edinburgh in midsummer. We talked. I don't know whether I was ever actually under hypnosis. But, whatever Bill did to me, it worked. On 26 July, in Helsinki's Olympic stadium, I broke Rowe's British record – not just broke it, obliterated it. In one enormous leap, I had improved the record and my record by more than 2 feet. I would go into the Olympic Games in Munich a month later as the British record holder at 20.18 metres (66 feet 2½ inches).

Breaking that record was like climbing a mountain. I had reached the summit and everything that followed was anti-climactic. My season had revolved round breaking the record. I had not expected to win the Olympic title that year, and had set myself another target. But, when the Olympics came, I had expected at least to qualify for the final. Eighteen throwers did, but not me. I threw a pitiful 18.94 metres (62 feet 1¾ inches), 4 feet down on my performance just a month earlier. My best putt would have placed me eighth. What I did left me twentieth. I was beginning to wonder whether I would ever bring home a medal.

6

The Strong Arm of the Law

The police force was a natural choice of career for Geoff Capes. A village yobbo he might have been, but he had never put himself on the wrong side of the law, and his grandfather, uncle and three elder brothers had all joined before him. One brother has since risen to the rank of chief inspector. Another owns a security company which provides bodyguards for the famous.

He applied to join in 1969, making it clear when he did that he wished to pursue his career as an athlete. No one made any promises on that score, but ultimately the most senior officers, recognizing his value to their public relations, gave him enormous assistance.

Initially, Police Constable 222 was stationed at Peterborough, doing the normal shift work of the average constable. In 1972 he was given a rural beat as the junior half of the two-man police force at Wittering. Wittering is a small village on the A1, notable only for its RAF station and the close proximity of Burghley House, stately home of the Marquis of Exeter, then president of the International Amateur Athletic Federation.

Finally he became PC 444 ('it was my only promotion'), attached to police headquarters at Huntingdon, responsible for cadet training and an instructor in physical education and police duty.

Many colleagues regarded it as a sinecure. On one of his annual reports, a senior officer wrote in the column for 'dress', 'Only ever seen in tracksuits.' But few of the cadets who passed through his hands would agree. They would remember him more as Chris Brasher described him in the Observer *in 1976:*

'He is very mild and quiet, except when driving on the police

41

cadets of Cambridgeshire who are in his charge. On Thursday he was polishing them up – and polishing some of them off – before the Police Cadet National Athletic Championships at Derby. When one of them collapsed gasping on the grass he yelled, 'You're not knackered. It's all in the mind. There is no pain. There is no pain.' And to another who had just run a half-mile in 2 minutes 35 seconds, 'Those fags will be the death of you, you wet weed. Don't you know there's a twelve-year-old girl – a girl, who's run a half-mile in 2 minutes 8 seconds?'

The police force, however, made considerable concessions to Geoff's sporting ambitions, allowing him enormous latitude in his duties. For ten years, in every branch of the media, he was, quite simply, always 'Geoff Capes, the policeman. . . .'

Police Review published a letter from a police wife complaining of my behaviour in a televised Super Stars Team contest. The cameras had picked up my foul; they didn't show the twenty or so fouls committed against me, and they didn't show the incident in which I was on the ground and getting kicked. And, because I was Geoff Capes the policeman, rather than Geoff Capes the shot putter, I was pilloried.

I knew there was resentment from other policemen about the time off I was having. What people never realized was that I was public property. I could be committed for twenty-four hours a day, every day. When I appeared on television in shorts and vest, I was still a policeman, and judged as a policeman. When I received invitations, I was expected to have a good reason if I turned them down, because I would be representing the police.

Usually the real reason was lack of time. Every evening of my week and every weekend was booked. I coached at St Ives four evenings each week – local kids as well as others from further afield who would stay at my house. I played in charity matches, took paraplegic kids to the seaside, turned out for athletic sponsors and Olympic sponsors. I was busy sixteen hours a day, and the sufferers were my family and my own hobbies, not the police.

The police was a vehicle for my athletics. I don't deny that. I never tried to hide it from them. My two chief constables, Drayden Porter and more recently Victor Gilbert, were fantastically helpful. Gilbert was the most down-to-earth senior copper you could hope to meet. He would go fishing, just like I do, and he would talk to the likes of me, an ordinary PC. Neither of them ever put obstacles in my way. It was help and guidance all the way. And I tried to put as much back as I took.

I was so keen to compete in the annual National Police Championships that, on one occasion, I arrived in Athens at three o'clock in the morning to join the rest of the British team for an international match. I had competed in the police event the previous afternoon. I appeared in national recruitment advertising and did an enormous amount of PR work – speaking, representing, that sort of thing.

And I think I was a pretty good copper. For five or six years I was on the normal beat work and then on a rural panda patrol, and I had the advantage that I was good with kids.

Yob is only boy spelt backwards. I was one myself once. I recognized that a yob was only a boy with nothing to do. I'd been in their shoes. I could cope with kids. I didn't have to book them. I talked their language. They respected me.

Okay, so I didn't have any paper qualifications. That's been the cause of the slight chip on my shoulder. But I reckoned that I was better suited to grass-roots police work than university graduates. Common sense is a large part of police work.

Of course, there was resentment about the time I spent away on my glamorous trips. I would have got that in any line of work. But, for Britain to compete in international amateur sport, the country needs jobs which give flexibility. I did my share of police work, and the majority of my colleagues understood that. Those who didn't work with me were those who didn't understand. They were the trouble-makers, the petty-minded who would continuously do things to show they were my superiors. Superior! Never. Senior, yes, but never superior. But they were the ones who would object behind my back to my going to receptions and special events to which they and the average copper weren't invited.

For an athlete, there are all sorts of problems attached to being a policeman – necessary restrictions that make life that little bit more difficult. Receiving commercial sponsorship, driving a sponsor's car, receiving gifts and awards – it's all against regulations, and I had to be careful what I did and seek guidance.

But the police *made* me. No doubt about that . . . they gave me a secure base in life and they taught me discipline. They made me a better sportsman and a better person. And having a wife and family at an early age gave me a reason for being disciplined, a reason for wanting to strive to get far beyond Holbeach, to make a name and make something of myself. And those two factors have shaped me. One thing you will always hear from people is that Geoff Capes is reliable. If he says he will turn up, he turns up, whether it is for an athletics meeting or a charity event.

Being 21 stone or more and enormously strong had its problems, too. I remember being involved in trouble at Peterborough United's ground, the London Road end. A kid hit me and I nicked him but, while I had hold of him, another kid tried to rescue him. So I banged the two together and took them from the ground.

Two weeks later, in court, all dressed up in their best suits and with mum and dad behind them, you wouldn't recognize them as the two hooligans at the match. And you should have heard the defence solicitor.

'Is it right, Mr Capes, that you weigh 21 stone, that you do boxing, weightlifting and judo?'

'Yes, sir.'

'And you're telling us that these two young boys assaulted you?'

'Yes, sir.'

'I put it to you, Mr Capes, that you used excessive force.'

I put it back to him that he had never been to the London Road end and been involved in a punch-up, but the magistrate shut me up. 'If I had wanted to use my strength to excess on your clients,' I said finally, 'they would not be fit to be here today.'

They were bound over for a year, but the whole incident was typical of the suspicion with which my size was regarded. There was another occasion in Peterborough when two women went wild outside a Chinese restaurant and started attacking the owner's car.

Because they were women, I had to call for the assistance of a woman constable. Two constables were sent, and they were no help. The two women leapt off the car and laid them out. The situation was becoming a farce. The police were being made fools of. People were laughing. So I grabbed both women by their hair, pulled them off the car and put them in the panda car. I was scratched, kicked and had my hair pulled. They even used the car's fire extinguisher on me. But I got into trouble later for manhandling women.

Capes was to figure prominently in the hunt for the Cambridge rapist. He did not catch him, and never once saw him, but there is one undergraduate who will never forget the part Capes played in the episode.

Capes, literally, went under cover. It was John Goodbody, a Fleet Street journalist who was then a mature student at Trinity College, who uncovered him one night. Goodbody, a third Dan black belt and the university judo coach, had taken a night-time job of protecting one of the women's colleges during the rapist scare. Each evening he jogged from his own rooms to take up his sentry duties.

One evening, jogging alone between an avenue of trees, he was startled from his thoughts of D. H. Lawrence by a disembodied voice hailing him. 'Hey, Goodbody, up here,' it repeated.

There, above him, sitting among the branches of a tree, was Capes, all 6 feet 5 inches and 22 stone of him, keeping a lookout for suspects. 'It was,' Goodbody recalls, 'probably the most ridiculous sight of my life.'

The best thing the police gave me was flexible working hours, so I could fit in my training. There was a period when I used to drive to the back of a gym, turn my personal wireless up loud and do my weight training in full uniform. Then I was still ready to answer any calls quickly.

At Wittering there was a well-equipped gym which I used, just round the corner at the RAF base, and at Huntingdon the facilities at the police headquarters were excellent. In those ways the police was a perfect training ground for an athlete.

In the end, the police and I parted company friends. It coincided with the debate over whether or not British athletes should participate in the Moscow Olympics, but that was not the only reason for my departure. With all the cutbacks, the steady flow of cadets coming through my hands had dried up – there were too few to justify my job. I knew that, after that Olympic year, I wouldn't have a role – and I couldn't see myself going back on a beat. I had done my share of that and the thought of a second dose didn't appeal greatly. It's something all police constables have to go through but, given the choice, not many would opt for it – and having been round the world several times during my shot-putting career and seen how the other half lives, I didn't fancy the lack of excitement one bit.

When the Moscow issue came up, I was already thinking about my future. There was no direct pressure on me. What little there was locally and nationally, through petty-minded councillors and members of the police committee, was soaked up by the chief constable. He never once let me feel the pressure.

Moscow just brought the matter to a head. I am as

sick as the next athlete about political pressure in sport. It is one thing after another these days – walk-outs, boycotts, bans, and all in the name of politics. Never does it have anything to do with sport itself.

But I was a policeman, and my local authority was Conservative, and the Conservative government was against athletes going to Moscow. I could see that my chief constable was in an impossible position. So, knowing that I wanted to go, I started to think about alternative employment, and Carter Pocock, the Reebok sportswear distributor, came up with an offer.

My chief told me not to worry about Moscow. 'You do what I say,' he said, but in the end I wanted to save him embarrassment. I handed in my ticket. It was the end of April. Any later might have interfered with my Olympic preparations. As it was, I could leave before the end of May, ease myself into a new job and still keep training.

The move did not stop the pressure against my going to the Moscow Olympics. There were still the letters; I filed all of them. More than half supported my desire to compete; some were against it, and some were extreme in their opposition.

An extract from one will demonstrate just how extreme the opposition could be. How about the letter from 'students of a Rotherham Comprehensive School' which was signed 'the True British Student' and written on the torn pages of an exercise book:

We think you are a traitor to England by going to the Olympic Games. You are only thinking of your big-headed self. If you go to Moscow, don't come back.

Another accused me of eating enough food daily to feed fifty starving children. Another more reasoned letter called on me to make an individual sacrifice.

But why only athletes? Why not businessmen? Why should they trade with Moscow when we could not compete there? Why should British companies be allowed to set up offices there in the very month a Prime Minister was calling on athletes to boycott the country? It was so

47

much sanctimonious, hypocritical humbug. And we have all seen now the enormous difference the absence of the United States, West Germany and a few other countries made to the people of Afghanistan!

Temporary boycotts do not work. They have been shown to fail so often now that I wonder any politician bothers with them. The African boycott of Montreal did not stop the New Zealand rugby team going to South Africa. Who remembers which countries boycotted the 1956 Olympics, and why? But they did. Who remembers which country boycotted the European Athletic Championships in 1969? But one did. All boycotts of this kind are pointless.

As part of a total expression of our feelings about the invasion of Afghanistan, sport might have played its part. On its own it was a useless, futile exercise. We went, a good number of athletes won and Mrs Thatcher ended up congratulating them in Parliament.

But what had she done for the athletes? Sue Reeve had had to go on official strike to get there, Joslyn Hoyte-Smith and Bernie Ford had lost money by having to take unpaid leave, and a lot of people in a lot of countries had lost the chance of a lifetime. And for what?

The governments of this country, whatever their colour and creed, do nothing for sport. They hardly recognize it exists. I can thank the butchers Dewhurst for helping me for many years with my food bills, Ford Motor Company for loaning me a car, ITT for helping throwers at one stage, on anonymous Greek businessman for sending me to America, and, most recently, the independent Sports Aid Foundation for giving me the money to train abroad. But I cannot remember one penny I have received which I owe directly to the government.

In 1980 the government received what they deserved in return. Nothing.

7

Record Breaking

The start of 1973 did nothing to reassure Geoff that he could be a winner. I remember his despondency, sitting apart at the official reception which followed the European Indoor Championships in Rotterdam that year. He had finished seventh, Winch ninth. That night all the fears and frustrations poured from him.

'I've got all it takes – the height, the power, the technique; I even go into that circle every time convinced that something big is going to happen, that it's going to go our 68 or 69 feet. But there's something missing.

'Perhaps I shouldn't have taken my wife on holiday for a week before these championships, but how can I say that to her when it's the first time she has had a holiday in four years?

'Sure, you can say Komar, the Olympic champion, is thirty-seven and I'm only twenty-three. But I've been British number one now for two years and what have I to show for it? A load of cups, shields, and medals that mean nothing – just presents. Here was a real medal for the taking and I fouled it up. That hurts.'

He was being severe on himself. Jaroslav Brabec, the Czech, had had to throw 20.28 metres – 10 centimetres further than Capes's British record – to win the title. Capes's training was going well; his wife Gillian had deserved that holiday. There was nothing wrong, as the next eighteen months were to prove. He was on the verge of the greatest two years of his career.

Until you have won something, you are just another good athlete. I was Commonwealth record holder and

49

British record holder, but I hadn't won a title that mattered yet.

That winter I was training six days a week, only resting on Mondays, and fitting everything around a full-time job as the village policeman at Wittering. Tuesday would be weights, Wednesday weights and throwing, Thursday exercises and weights, Friday throwing, Saturday a weights competition and a 3 mile run, and more throwing and weights on Sunday. Each session lasted between two and three hours. I was 310 pounds, but it was all muscle.

Of course, that amount of work every day demands phenomenal energy, and at the same time I had to keep my weight up. So, most of the time I was not training or being a policemen, I was eating. Gillian had to serve up about five meals a day. I used to say it was a little and often but, by most men's standards, it was a lot and often.

A newspaper reporter came to Wittering one day to calculate what I was eating in a day. Their list consisted of: cornflakes, seven pints of milk, two tins of pilchards, three cartons of cottage cheese, two loaves, a leg of lamb, two steaks, twelve eggs, 1 pound of butter, a jar of orange juice, a tin of baked beans, a rice pudding, a pot of honey, a grapefruit and two tins of tuna fish.

It was not like that every day. The menu changed, but the quantity was typical enough. And, on a policeman's wage, balancing the family budget was a losing battle. I was dipping into my small amount of savings just to feed myself.

Newspaper readers probably became tired of my pleas for sponsorship. But, when you are lifting sometimes as much as 150 tons in a single training session – about the equivalent of twenty double-decker buses (but not all at once!) – you need fuel.

In many ways, 1973 was a turning point. For the first time I found myself a sponsor – Jack Myers, a London businessman, He paid for a steak every day. Later, a group of businessmen and a meat trade journal paid my complete weekly meat bill. It was between £15 and £20 – and, remember, that was seven or eight years ago.

Finally, J. H. Dewhurst Ltd, the butchers, came to the rescue. They allowed me to have up to £20's worth of prime steak every week from their local branch, and then Unigate weighed in with £5's worth of dairy produce each week.

British athletes in the mid-1970s were competing not only against the best in the world but against the greater support other countries gave those athletes. In Finland, from the start of the seventies, athletes were given monthly financial support according to their standard, and they were allowed to use a training camp in the south of Spain, where accommodation and food were free, whenever they wished. Their return air fares to Spain were also paid. The West Germans had the Sporthilfe scheme with its large cash grants from a private enterprise group and, as one would expect, athletes in Eastern Europe never wanted for anything.

In Britain we had to make do with few facilities and paltry support. It can be no surprise that far fewer youngsters go for the technical throwing and jumping events. It is so much easier to become a runner. Any bit of road or park will do, and there are few towns which have not laid a track of some description. But how many have pole-vault run-ups or shot circles? And even in 1980 there are not more than a handful which have indoor throwing nets for the winter.

There have been many occasions when throwing in winter has meant taking a bucket of hot water with me to the circle, and dipping the shot and my throwing hand into it before each throw. And there cannot be a thrower in Britain who has not started a training session by mopping the circle dry. It is all part of the apprenticeship. It is no wonder that throwers in our country feel like second-class citizens. Not only is there pitiful media coverage of field events, but we are considered less important even within our own sport.

I cannot count the number of times I have heard

meeting organizers suggesting that the hammer competition should be held outside the main area. Even the shot circle at Crystal Palace was positioned badly until we demanded that it should be moved in front of the main stand. Britain is a harrier nation. We put track men on pedestals and worship them.

Okay, so we have had great track runners. We have also had many great field-event athletes – Lynn Davies, Arthur Rowe, Mary Rand, Mary Peters. Yet there have been times when you would think from reading the newspapers that there were only one or two athletes in the country. And they have always been runners.

In 1973 I competed in 126 outdoor competitions. That is more than two each week every week of the year. Often weeks went by without one competition, and in others I would be competing on Wednesday, Friday, Saturday and Sunday. Some of the runners come out half a dozen times a year. Sometimes you have the ridiculous situation of an athlete arriving at the Olympic trials for his first competition of the summer. That's not what athletics is all about.

I lost just two of those competitions outdoors in 1973. Both were to Hartmut Briesenick. The first was in Leipzig when Britain competed against East Germany. The second was in Edinburgh at the Europa Cup Final. I was third, and I had wrist trouble that day. It was my first Europa Cup final – Britain's first for eight years – and what an occasion! Chris Monk won the 200 metres, Andy Carter the 800 metres, Frank Clement the 1500 metres, Brendan Foster the 5000 metres and Alan Pascoe the 400 metres hurdles.

The throwers chipped in their bit too. I beat the Soviet Union's Valeri Voikin for third, Bill Tancred beat another Russian for third in the discus, Dave Travis was fourth in the javelin and, although Barry Williams was only fifth in the hammer, he was a lot less than a metre behind the second-placed man.

Mind you, the weather must have helped us that day. It was cold, wet and windy, just the kind in which we were all so used to training. Those poor Eastern Europeans with their centrally heated indoor facilities did not know what had hit them.

Before that match I had broken my own British record three times in the space of seventeen days during July – at Crystal Palace on the 14th by just 9 centimetres, by a further 7 centimetres five days later in Athens, and finally to 20.47 metres (67 feet 2 inches) in East Berlin on the 31st.

The reason for so many competitions in one year was the strange calendar for athletics in 1973. The season never ended. In late September, when normally we take a break, we had the Commonwealth Games trials at Crystal Palace to select the team for the Games in Christchurch, New Zealand, the following January and February.

I decided at the start of 1973 to compete straight through until Christchurch. Many of the runners were taking a break from competition, pouring a great many miles of endurance training into a shortened winter programme before the Games the following January, but, after the Commonwealth trials in late September, I made sure that, wherever there was an event, I was there too.

The final competition before departure was at Crystal Palace, outdoors, in the first week of January. It was snowing when I arrived, and cold enough to freeze the fingers together, but it would have needed more than that to hold me. This was my year. I felt it in my fitness. I intended to start it as I wanted it to continue, and I did – with a new Commonwealth and British record of 20.59 metres (67 feet 6¾ inches). How many times, I wonder, have British records been broken outdoors in the first week of January?

Four days later, we left for New Zealand. It was a charter flight, and there were English and Scottish team members on board, about 340 in all, lying all over the seats and gangways like a defeated army. It was one of the most horrible experiences of my life.

I hate flying, and with every flight that hate has

grown. It began with a bad landing at Amsterdam on a LOT Airways flight from Warsaw, and turned to paranoia after the athlete John Cooper was among the hundreds killed in the DC10 crash in Paris. I lose weight on every flight. On take-off and landing I sit gripping the arms of the seats until my knuckles go white and the sweat pours off me. I barely relax even when we are in flight, and the slightest turbulence sets me off again. I remember screaming on a plane between Auckland and Christchurch during a storm.

British Airways were so concerned when they heard of my fears that they sent me a special tape recording which was supposed to calm me. It did not work. When they investigated me in 1979 the Inner Game people – a group of head shrinkers (see page 110) – said they had never seen a more screwed-up guy. Everybody tells me that flying is one of the safest forms of travel and that, according to the law of averages, the risk of a crash is very low. But the more you fly the less the averages are on your side. That's how I reason it, and the fear has cost me hundreds of competitions.

I drove to Turin once for an England international match against the United States, and I have frequently taken a boat to meetings in Scandinavia. In 1980, when the Sports Aid Foundation gave me money for Stuart and myself to train for a week in Spain, I set off three days early with Gillian in the car, drove to Plymouth, caught the ferry to San Sebastian and drove across Spain to our camp. Stuart and his wife flew. Curiously, Gillian is also scared stiff of planes.

I have had to come to terms with flying in order to continue as an international athlete, but I never relish the prospect. Before the 1976 Olympic Games in Montreal, I was so worried about flying there that I arranged to join a Polish liner at Tilbury for the eight-day voyage across the Atlantic and down the St Lawrence Seaway. I even had my own weights put on board for that voyage. Anything was better than flying.

People have suggested that I suffer from claustrophobia, because I am never so bad when I am up front with the pilot and can see where we are going. But I am not claustrophobic in any other situation, and I think what happens to me in the pilot's cabin is merely reassurance that all is well and everybody is doing their job there.

That flight to Christchurch was my first long flight – more than twenty-eight hours via Bahrain, Singapore and Melbourne, four take-offs and four landings. Brendan Foster said later that I had spent most of those twenty-eight hours visiting the cockpit to make sure the pilot was awake. He was right. I hardly slept a wink. Others danced, sang, played cards or made a bid for membership of the Six Mile High Club, but I just clung on.

Thirty minutes out of Christchurch, we were ordered to change into our uniforms. When the 747 landed, what emerged was a dry-cleaned, laundered, shaved and suited team with the reddest eyes humanly possible. We should have frightened the natives but they had turned out their own warriors to meet the invasion – a band of Maoris running towards us, sticking out their tongues and waving axes at us.

Naturally, the runners got behind the throwers for protection. It was a fun start to the trip – and just about the last time there that the throwers got on as a team.

8

Big is Beautiful

Throwers are a strange breed. They are the big men, the strong men, and yet they group themselves like a threatened species, each protecting the other. I well remember a small group of them in the Five Bridges Hotel at Gateshead after a reception, all desperately trying to ignore a little man who was bad-mouthing Capes. The little guy was putting his head in the lion's mouth but the lion was doing his utmost to develop lockjaw. They were quite simply scared of their own strength and its potential for damage should they lose their control.

Yet strangely, when throwers do lose their cool, it is often with each other.

Mike Winch is the only thrower in Britain who has given me any serious competition since 1971. If there is anybody who is more fanatical about shot putting than I am, it is Mike. He is obsessed by it, and will not stand any criticism of it. Over the years, I think our rivalry has given the event an enormous boost in Britain, and we have even become firm allies in its cause.

But in 1973 we were at each other's throats. Mike had improved enormously during the winter of 1972–3. In Madrid he had thrown 19.42 metres (63 feet 8¾ inches) indoors – nearly 3 feet further than he had ever thrown outdoors. And during 1973 he pushed his personal record outdoors up six times until he threw 19.65 metres (64 feet 5¾ inches), in Athens. I had to putt a British record that day to beat him.

What got up my nose about him was his constant emphasis of his smallness. He is 5 feet 11½ inches and now weighs about 230 pounds. That is a bit short for a top-class shot putter. Al Feuerbach is only 6 feet tall but most of the top shot putters have been taller. Matson is 6 feet 6½ inches. Barishnikov is 6 feet 6¼ inches. Beyer is 6 feet 4¾ inches, Stahlberg 6 feet 4½ inches. Working in a 7 foot circle has its disadvantages for a big man but this is more than cancelled out by the advantages a few extra inches of height gives you. Of the top ten all-time throwers on the world list, Feuerbach is the shortest, and the next smallest is George Woods at 6 feet 2 inches.

But Mike kept emphasizing that for his height he was the best in Britain. It was true but irrelevant. It's like Linsey Macdonald asking for a 10 metre start in the Olympic final because the other girls were taller and more powerful. By the time we reached Christchurch I regarded him not so much as a rival but as a pain in the backside.

Typically, the management was so ignorant about personal relationships that the throwers had to share rooms with each other. What they forget is that people in the same event may be in the same national team but, when it comes to gold medals, they are competing against each other.

Winch was roomed with Barry Williams, the hammer thrower, and soon Barry was being drawn into the dispute between Mike and me. Since we were always having a go at one another, Barry could not avoid it. Mike and I trained at different times, and conflicting reports about our performances circulated. His supporters would let it be known that he had achieved 68 feet in training, and I would tell others I had done 70 feet. It was that petty. But one of my throws was an indisputable British and Commonwealth mark of 20.64 metres (67 feet 8¾ inches). I travelled to Timaru just a week after we arrived in New Zealand, a beautiful spot where the sea was bluer than I had ever seen it and the welcome was the warmest. I loved the place and I did it justice with the only record of the meeting.

When I arrived back in Christchurch, others were competing in a pre-Games meeting in the stadium. I went along as a spectator. It was all festive stuff, nothing too serious. The throwers not competing had the odd beer, and were jocular, but nobody was rowdy. We made the occasional unhelpful comment and sarcasm to each other but it was all light-hearted stuff. That is, we thought it was.

What we did not appreciate was the great difficulty Barry was having with his technique. He could not get it right. Our comments were not helping. He was boiling up. When he made one mis-throw and nearly decapitated a judge, my loud remark started everybody laughing. It was the final straw for Barry. From 50 yards away, he stormed towards me.

'Don't you swear at me,' he said.

'Here, cool down with this,' I replied, splashing some beer in his direction.

At that point, Winch jumped into the argument. It was all verbal, nothing physical, but the press came to hear of it and before we knew it, the whole affair was a 'brawl in front of 30,000 people'.

What the press fortunately did not know was that it continued later back in the village. We were all in the dining room when another remark was made and suddenly we were throwing tables at each other. Other throwers separated us but word now got through to the management.

Doug Goodman, the team manager, called us before him and threatened to send us home. Had the management seen the trouble brewing earlier and been on top of the problem, it would have never reached that point.

But, back home, it was out of hand already. My chief constable wanted to know what I was doing, and Mike's mother wrote to the newspapers saying that her boy was an angel and that he was the only thrower not on drugs.

What nobody seemed to appreciate was that people

who would be competing against each other in five days'
time were having to live together. Even friendships are
forgotten in that situation. You're out to win the same
honour. Mike and I had seen eye to eye on virtually
nothing – we argued about technique, size, strength, and
still he could not accept that the name of our game was
throwing a 16 pound ball furthest. But I still respect him
as a fine thrower. It was only the tension that comes
before competition which had made us both a little
excited.

The newspapers had now escalated our verbal scrap
into full-scale war. Everybody wanted their say about it,
and it made out relationship far worse.

The opportunity to put all that bad feeling into a
competition against him almost disappeared before the
event. I went to the beach with some boat surfers and
they took me out about 1000 yards in one of their boats.
There were about eight of us, and they brought us in
with the surf. I was excited but terrified: I had not told
them that I could not swim well. Only when the boat
lurched so far to one side I thought it would capsize did I
yell the truth to them. Then they grabbed hold of me and
helped me to the beach.

After that, not even the news that Winch had thrown
over 66 feet in training two days before could frighten
me. I was so ready for competition I could not sleep. I
felt such strength in me that I could have lent Winch a
share. The chief constable turned up trumps again with a
telegram wishing me good luck. After the anxiety I had
caused him in the press a few days earlier it was a
generous touch.

Our competition did not come until the final day, 2
February 1974. For me, it was the first major Games in
which I had had a real chance of winning, the first in
which I had been the favourite. And, for the first time in
a major event, I did not waste the chance. With my first
throw, I blasted out a new British and Commonwealth
record of 20.74 metres (68 feet ½ inch), a New Zealand
all-comers record.

All my pent-up anger went into that throw – anger at all the comments, the stories in the press, Mike's mother's letter. You need that to build the aggression. I was even saying to Mike, 'Hi, there, how's your mummy?' I loved it. I was constructing a big hate thing against him, psyching myself up to beat him. It was him or me. He came back with 63 feet 7 inches, but there was no real opposition. I changed to a different shot for the last round and hurled it out more than 69 feet, but it was a foul.

I had won my first major title. The mental block had been removed. I felt good enough to win anything now. I had not just won, but won with a record throw. I could not wait for my next chance.

We flew home the next day, another harrowing experience, but I was so full of myself now that it hardly bothered me. Only eighteen days after reaching home, I was competing again, this time at Cosford for an indoor international match against Spain. I was still 'hot'. There the shot flew 20.82 metres (68 feet 3¾ inches), a British and Commonwealth indoor record and my best throw indoors or out. This throw was also a European indoor record – the first time any Briton had achieved that since Arthur Rowe in 1962. I was ranked number one in Europe.

Next came the European Indoor Championships in Gothenburg, Sweden, in early March, and a chance to win my first major European title. I was full of confidence, suntanned, fit and competitively sharp. Britain only sent a small team of about five athletes.

The top man there to beat that year was the East German Heinz Joachin Rothenburg who has an outdoor best of 69 feet 11½ inches. In the warm-up I let loose and threw almost 22 metres. I just froze. I looked up at Stuart and he could not believe it. Ron Pickering sitting with him in the commentary position could not believe it.

Rothenburg opened the competition with a throw of 68 feet 5 inches for a new European indoor record – just a bit over an inch better than my mark at Cosford. I thought, 'Here we go, what a great competition this is going to be.' I was in the mood. Previously his challenge might have unsettled me, but now I was excited about the contest.

I was so excited I was shaking. I couldn't believe that in that warm-up throw, I'd been over the world record. I opened with 20.95 metres (68 for 8¾ inches), a new European, Commonwealth and British record. Rothenburg lost interest and dropped back, but I finished the competition with three more 68 feet plus throws, my best series to date.

So that was it. 1974 was not three months old and I was Commonwealth champion and European indoor champion. But there was a new challenge on the horizon. His name was Al Feuerbach. He was American. The previous May he had set the world record at 21.82 metres (71 feet 7 inches). He had been fifth in the 1972 Olympics, was the reigning American champion and was to become, without any shadow of doubt, the most consistent American thrower throughout the 1970s.

Feuerbach came to Britain for the first time that year in late May. It was the Philips International meeting at Crystal Palace, and his opposition was Winch and myself. It was to be an epic, and it was the start of a competitive series which gripped British athletic crowds across the country that summer.

What was so wonderful was having a man of Feuerbach's calibre to challenge on my home ground. He was the world-record holder. For too long Mike and I had been fighting each other. It was beginning to damage us both; we were thinking negatively. We were thinking about beating each other, not about throwing further. Feuerbach changed all that. That first contest began slowly. It was a cold evening. None of us hit it right in the first round. In the second, I had a big one, but four of the judges ruled it a foul. The one who was watching at the time thought it was okay. The others claimed my left foot was on the top of the stop board.

Then, wallop, Mike pulls out the first 67 foot throw of

his life – 20.43 metres. Flash, bang, wallop, the little old warning light comes on in my mind. I can remember taking off my tracksuit bottoms, something I rarely did. Then the competition started. I threw 20.81 metres (68 feet 3¼ inches), a new British and Commonwealth record, the fourth outdoors that year. It was not good enough. Feuerbach threw over 69 feet to win.

Four days later at Crystal Palace we met again. This time it was my turn to win. Again it was a British and Commonwealth record of 20.90 metres (68 feet 7 inches). The pace was hotting up. Al gave an interview to *Athletics Weekly* in which he said my basic throwing principles, the plant of both feet and how I used them, was similar to the East German method. More important to me, Al said he thought I could throw 71 feet. It was a long time before he was proved right, but right he was.

Al went back to the United States after that competition, twice beat George Woods there and reached 69 feet 11 inches. So I knew that his defeat by me was nothing to do with any lack of form on his part. He was having a good year, and I beat him fair and square on the day. We met seven more times that summer, and he won six. But the challenge was good for me. On 19 June I broke the British record again at Crystal Palace with 68 feet 10¾ inches, the eleventh time in my life I had added to that record.

My fame was spreading. The University of Colorado in the United States contacted me to offer me a scholarship to study criminology – and, of course, compete as an athlete for them. It was my sixth offer from an American university that year and, for a boy who had not been fifteen when he left school and who did not have one paper qualification to his name, it was flattering. But I had a wife and by now two children, Lewis and Emma-Jane, and uprooting them for three years to live in a strange place on a student's scholarship did not appeal. For the sixth time I turned an offer down.

There were two highlights left for me. The first came at the British Games in August. I beat the British record again but more than that I became the first Briton to throw more than 70 feet – 70 feet 1½ inches, to be precise – and the first to throw over 21 metres – 21.37 metres – an improvement in one throw of more than a foot. And I had beaten Feuerbach for the second time in the process.

To throw 70 feet you have to concentrate only on the basics. Relax, right foot, left foot, one, two. When left foot is down, drive up, look for the sky. Left shoulder high, the whip-hip movement, accelerate with speed, arm movement fast. There's a final lunge, *snap*! It's all logical and easy but it only occasionally comes together. Then you feel nothing – and you have thrown 70 feet. When it happens, it seems the easiest throw of your life. And, because it feels easy, you know it is good. You hardly have to look for the mark.

What followed at the European Championships in Rome was perhaps less than I might have expected. I had beaten the defending champion Briesenick in a dual international against East Germany with a final round throw of 21.0 metres, and had also beaten his compatriot Rothenburg that year. But when it came to my third major championship of the year they both beat me. I had to settle for a bronze medal with a throw of 20.36 metres (66 feet 3¾ inches), with Briesenick winning with 67 feet 3 inches.

In one way I considered that I had failed. I had expected to win. But I had been competing virtually non-stop for twenty months, and at full stretch for eight months including three major events. No athlete alive could keep going at the top flat out for that long. None should even try. You can criticize me for spending too much time in minor competitions, but the series against Feuerbach was just as important to me and probably more important for the standing of the event in Britain. Had the European competitions been earlier in 1974 I might have won the gold. But I was happy with what I had achieved in a year.

It taught me too that you cannot be successful in

major championships while competing in every minor meet. I had had more than sixty competitions that year, and that wasn't good preparation for Rome.

At the end of the year the American magazine *Track and Field News,* which tends to favour Americans in its annual rankings, awarded me third place in the world. It was a fair calculation. Feuerbach had beaten me seven times out of nine, and Briesenick had beaten me when it counted. But I had jumped from twenty-third place the previous year. Nobody could argue about my improvement.

9

The Official Verdict

Nobody can dispute Capes's contribution to his sport. The Olympic Games in Moscow gave him his sixty-sixth appearance for Britain. He has made more for England and for Amateur Athletic Association representative teams. He has become a Southern Counties staff coach, acts as an examiner for prospective Board coaches, and organized, found sponsorship for and coached the Southern Shot Squad.

He has been team captain of British teams abroad, has promoted a highly successful international meeting in Spalding, and is coaching some of Britain's most outstanding juniors, including Tony Zaidman, Susan King and George Brocklebank, the most recent youth champions.

What Capes has never learnt is respect for the athletic authorities. He now serves on the committees of the International Athletes Club, the East Midlands Sports Council and the Sports Aid Foundation, but he has less time for his sport's own officials than he did for his childhood teachers.

There were times in the writing of this chapter when I imagined it would end up like the famous footballer Len Shackleton's opinions in his book on club directors – several blank pages. Most of what Capes feels about the national administrators of his sport, particularly in his early days, would contravene the laws of libel if they appeared in this book.

So, excuse the absence of names, but accept what he claims as the reality. In almost every case, I have confirmed his memory of incidents with others present. The opinions, of course, are his alone, but they reflect those of almost every international athlete for the past forty years who has spoken his mind.

In the past two years, a degree of professionalism has found its way into the administration of athletics in Britain. There are men now at the top who put the athletes first, who recognize that without the stars there would not be any television fees, sponsorship or revenue-producing crowds, and that the lower strata of the sport would suffer.

The ruling class of British athletics have drawn up a constitution which has created and perpetuated an autocracy. I call them the Black Hand Gang. Once you are a member, you are there until you die. Everybody looks after everybody else.

Until recently, the clubs were not even allowed to be heard at the annual meeting of the British Amateur Athletic Board. Even today, they are not allowed to cast a vote. It is government by officials, for officials, of the athletes.

The rules the officials make are for their own convenience and comfort. Take the rule about all athletes competing abroad needing a team manager to accompany them – a chaperon, if you like. That is just a subtle guarantee that the officials themselves have plenty of trips.

In 1972, when I was twenty-two, I went to Holland to compete. My nominated team manager was Vera Searle, an honorary official of the Women's Amateur Athletic Association. I went by boat; she went by plane. I never saw her.

I have now been to more than fifty countries. I know more about travelling than any official alive. I am also more capable of looking after myself than any official. Only in the last year or so have the Board begun to recognize it. But still they send managers with small groups of athletes who are perfectly capable of looking after themselves.

In the early part of my international career, officials even took their wives and sons on trips to international matches. There have been occasions when officials have been in the first-class section of planes while athletes sat in economy.

The waste was scandalous; officials hired private cars, held parties on the trips and entertained liberally out of the team's financial float. There were always cars waiting at airports for them and, once they had dumped you at the most basic hotel in town, off they would go to their official banquet.

For years it was a them-and-us team. Take the tickets at major Games. I've often gone to the village office or to our Olympic team chief for tickets for another sport and been told that one of the athletics team officials has taken the allocation for himself that day.

There was a time in Christchurch at the Commonwealth Games when I asked for an official car to take me to a training session. The car was not available. An English team official had commandeered it to go to a party.

Officials always have this superior attitude, conveying the impression that they set the example of what is right, and that we must all act like perfect Oxbridge Englishmen. But, when you have been on the international team for thirteen years as I have, you know better.

I've seen officials incapacitated with drink, not just officials but the team coaches. At Christchurch a British coach spent his time in bed with a champion from another country. He must have given her some good advice. She beat all the British girls to win the gold medal.

At one European indoor meeting I walked out one night and fell over the team doctor entwined with the physiotherapist on the bench. Okay, so the athletes aren't angels either, but we do not claim so-called positions of responsibility. We never make any claims to be paragons of virtue. But when one of the throwers, a soldier, was caught with a hotel manager's wife, the officials wrote to inform his commanding officer. The thrower was threatened with an overseas posting if it happened again.

I remember another team doctor who brought an

illegal flick knife through the British customs for his son. There was a time when a team manager distributed bottles of whisky to members of the team to take through customs for him to hand out to his friends among the officials in a Communist country.

There was the case of the missing case of whisky. It disappeared from the officials' quarters at a major championship. I was asked to find the thief. I soon found him, but I also found out that the whisky had not been given to the officials but was intended as a present to the team. So the thief's identity was never disclosed. He had only taken for the team what belonged to the team.

Just occasionally, the administration unearthed a good team manager by mistake. Jim Biddle was one. He was the director of physical education at Borough Road College in London. He was working throughout his life with young athletes. He understood them, and knew how and when to help .

The administration soon dumped him. He was not one of their old school. He was too close to the athletes. Jim was the best team manager Britain had had in ten years, but his face did not fit.

Most of the time we did not have proper team managers. We had to put up with the Board's honorary officials' doubling up so they could come on the trips. Some of them did not know one athlete from another. I remember one manager greeting sprinter Ian Matthews with the words 'Hello, Bob, how's your pole vaulting going?' Ian was Britain's number one sprinter at the time.

Basically, the difference between athlete and official was one of age. The officials thought all athletes were students on summer vacation with a family stipend. They still thought in terms of Lord Burghley and Harold Abrahams. It did not occur to them that there were athletes who had no money, who did not get paid if they did not work, who could not afford to compete here, there and everywhere at the whim of officials without being adequately compensated.

In 1980 they still paid us a top rate of 5p a mile for petrol, no more than a second-class rail fare even if every seat was taken and you had to stand from London to Edinburgh, and no allowance for a taxi, even if, as sometimes happened, your hotel was 3 miles from the station.

Until very recently, officials treated athletes like children. You will do it our way, or not at all. If I make a reasonable request I expect it to have reasonable consideration or I get bloody-minded. I have never asked for much. Back in 1975 I wanted the shot circle bang in front of the stand at Crystal Palace. The crowd wanted it, and I needed that kind of atmosphere. The great throwers appearing there from abroad deserved that sort of treatment. The organizers agreed in the end but if they hadn't I would have stayed away. This was the only treatment they understood.

There was another occasion when, for a Europa Cup match at Crystal Palace, I made the entirely reasonable request to stay nearby in the Queen's Hotel, instead of the hostel at the National Sports Centre. The hostel was always a soul-destroying place. The British Board refused. So I asked if I could use the hotel if I paid my own bill. No chance, they said; the team stays at the hostel and so do you. I didn't. I stayed at the Queen's. I'm an amateur athlete and I'm entitled to prepare as I want. I'm not being paid for my time and my efforts. It is my sport and I'm out to enjoy it. The hotel was full of the Russian team, and the Board didn't do a thing about it. The only way is to stand up to them or they will walk all over you.

Trouble flared up at the European Championships in Helsinki in 1971. We were fed up with the management but most of all we were concerned about the distribution of pocket money. Every athlete on an official team received a small daily amount to cover his out-of-pocket expenses. It has never been much, and in 1971 only $5 a day was permitted by the International Federation.

The British Board, in their generosity, offered us 50p.

We demanded £9 for the trip, twice what they were offering but half what the IAAF permitted. Alan Pascoe was the official team captain and he handed the officials a letter signed by every athlete.

But it was the hammer thrower Barry Williams who acted as the real spokesman. In front of all of us he simply said, 'May we have our proper per day expenses?' He was ordered to sit down by the team boss, Arthur Gold, and to be quiet. The next day we received our full entitlement. But they made Barry pay for it by not selecting him for the British team for at least a year.

The official reason was his behaviour the following day at the opening ceremony. Barry had stomach pains but was ordered to take part. Out in the centre arena, he felt so bad he sat down. He was still sitting down when the Finnish national anthem was played. He was physically sick but that was not an acceptable excuse.

In 1974, I was invited to the New Zealand Games that would take place the following January. It was a personal, verbal invitation from the New Zealand organizers. The former athlete and Northern Ireland official Maeve Kyle and her daughter Shauna were present when I received it. But the Board Secretary Arthur Gold nominated Bill Tancred for the trip in my place.

I was angry. I gave an interview in *Athletics Weekly* saying, 'No matter what Arthur Gold says, I know I was invited.' Three days later I received a letter from the British Board's solicitors demanding that I retract what I said – the inference was that Mr Gold was a liar.

I was very surprised because the letter was from the Board's solicitors rather than Mr Gold's. It must have cost the Board money to use solicitors for that purpose – money the sport could ill afford. And it gained them nothing. I passed the matter to the Police Federation solicitors and never heard another word.

Fortunately, nobody could leave me out of the team. There might have been other hammer throwers, but from 1971 no shot putter in Britain had been able to beat me. I was so far ahead of the pack they had to pick me.

I could afford to speak my mind, and frequently did so.

By August 1974, I had had an unbroken run of forty-six international matches for Britain. There was not a runner in the country who approached that number. Yet, when I ended that run by withdrawing from the match against Sweden because of fatigue, Arthur Gold was furious. Because I had competed in Edinburgh and Middlesbrough the previous weekend, he accused me of being 'tired from pot hunting'.

Of course, when it suits the officials, they can bend the rules better than anybody. In 1977, my wife and I were invited for a holiday in the best hotel in San Sebastian before the European Indoor Championships. For three days and nights, we enjoyed full board free of charge. Only when the rest of Britain's team arrived did I move out to join them. Those three days cost me nothing. I can only assume the British Board footed the bill. It was against the amateur rules, but it suited the Board for me to compete in the championships.

What the athletes need most from officials is support. We want to feel that they are on our side, that, if there are problems, they will speak for us and defend us. At last this is beginning to happen. For the first time, in 1980, we had team officials who were experienced former athletes and were not doubling up on other officials' duties.

That was the root of the problem in the past. Marea Hartman was treasurer of the British Board, secretary of the Women's AAA and chairman of the IAAF women's commission. She was also the women's team manager. Arthur Gold was the men's team manager or, more often, the grander chef d'équipe – a sort of boss of bosses He was also secretary of the British Board. I remember watching him at the European Championships in Rome, stopwatch in hand, helping to select the four to run in the relay team. It was like Ted Croker advising Ron Greenwood who should be England's goalkeeper.

What is necessary is a 'St Valentine Day's massacre' of

the old school, the Black Hand Gang. Athletics needs a clean-out of their generation. Let them accept positions on the IAAF and the European AA. Let them work for their knighthoods on the Sports Council.

At team level we want professionals. Thankfully, we are beginning to get them. In 1980, Nick Whitehead, who has won an Olympic medal, was the overall manager; Lynn Davies and Mary Peters, both Olympic champions of recent vintage, were the individual team managers. It brought a breath of fresh air. Long may it last.

10

Montreal and Before

The 1972 Olympic Games had been an experience for Capes. He had been an apprentice Olympian, learning the ropes, discovering the problems, finding out what it was like to live in an Olympic Village and compete in the atmosphere of the greatest sporting show on earth.

But in 1976 he was expected to be among the medallists. For the three years before those Games in Montreal he was among the best in the world. He had matured into a reliable and consistent performer at the highest level. The build-up to those Games fully supported the widely held opinion that he could win Britain's first Olympic medal in the shot.

I was the world number seven in 1975 but I cannot remember much about it. It was a mediocre year for shot putting, and for me. My best was 68 feet 3 inches. It says a lot about the way athletes react to a year without major competitions. When there is nothing to aim at, you feel yourself go over to automatic pilot. You just cruise. Nobody hit 70 feet in 1975 anywhere in the world.

I cruised better than most. I was consistently around 68 feet, and I won the silver medal in the European Indoor Championships in Katowice, Poland, losing the title I had won a year earlier to the Bulgarian Stove. I was unwell at the time but my mood was not improved by the post-competition celebrations.

Arthur Gold, who was with the team management, had promised to buy champagne for any winners. 'Ah,

Geoff,' he said greeting me. 'A silver medal, yes. A glass of Coke for you.'

It may have been intended as a joke, but I did not get to see the champagne. He and I have never been the greatest of chums. We come from opposite ends of the social spectrum. Throwers are not his cup of tea and outspoken throwers are the worst kind in his opinion. He comes from a generation which expects athletes to run, jump and throw – and allow officials to govern.

He never accepted that athletes are what athletics is all about, and certainly not that they could possibly have anything useful to offer. Suggestions were regarded as criticisms, and there was a perceptible barrier between him and the athletes.

Credit where it's due . . . he did save me from considerable embarrassment on one occasion. I had changed English money on the black market in Poland. The rate was three times as high as the official exchange rate in our hotel – enough to convert our miserly pocket money into enough to buy a decent present for the wife.

When I returned to the hotel, a plain-clothes policeman was waiting. He questioned me, and said I must accompany him to his office. I refused; Arthur was called and, at his most diplomatic, pointed out the political repercussions which might follow any action against a visiting athlete. The policeman relented.

From a personal viewpoint, the repercussions for me would have been far more damaging. My own police force would have had to discipline me at the very least. I might even have ended up in a Polish labour camp! Arthur is fond of reminding me of the incident when I criticize management.

Of course, officials could tell tales on the athletes. A lot of things happen on the way to an athletics meeting. Nobody is going to claim that athletes are any more moral and any less fun-loving than the average young people. But sport is our hobby; it should be fun.

We complain about management when we feel they are ruining that fun. Too often we feel we are part of some military exercise, an expeditionary force. Do this, don't do that, left, right, left, right, blazers on, off . . . oh get lost! It's all this representing Britain thing. I've done it more than any British athlete. Of course it is an honour to be the person representing all the other athletes and people in your country. But athletes are individuals. We are not training three hours a day only for Britain. It's for ourselves as well.

The Olympics would still be the Olympics if the athletes represented nobody but themselves. It is an occasion for individuals. So what right has anybody to tell us what we can and cannot do? We need officials to enable us to compete in optimum conditions, free from the pressures of having to organize transport, facilities and accommodation, and deal with the irritating items we would otherwise have to attend to ourselves. We do not need officers to command us or control us.

A manager should be somebody appointed to manage the affairs of the team. Athletes who have had the willpower, dedication, self-control and maturity to reach the peak of their chosen sports should not need a boss. They are the self-motivators.

Not that anybody could accuse me of not flying the flag. I have turned out more often than others, and have been a consistent point scorer for the national team. That year in the Europa Cup final in Nice, there were six British winners, and I was one of them. David Jenkins won the 400 metres, Steve Ovett the 800, Foster the 5000, Pascoe the 400 metres hurdles and Britain won the 4 × 400 metres relay.

My win was Britain's first field event victory in a Europa Cup final. It was still Britain's only win in that department when I retired. Of the world's best throwers I beat the East German Rothenburg, the Russian Volkin and the West German Reichenbach, with a putt of 20.80 metres, far ahead of Rothenburg's best for second place of 20.33 metres.

Unfortunately, Britain's other field-event men had a disastrous day, all finishing seventh or eighth, and that held Britain back in fourth place overall, even though we had the most individual winners.

1975 ended less happily. I injured my ankle and was on crutches for Christmas. But there was a special present waiting for me . . . the trip of a lifetime.

I needed a fresh challenge, something to draw the best from me. It was Olympic year, and my summer season would start later than usual. I wanted exciting winter events, and where better to look for them than the United States?

I had read so much about their indoor circuit that I wanted to experience it. Leave was no problem. The police were marvellous about it. But where could I get the money to pay for such a trip? The answer, when it finally came, was a Greek businessman in London. He wanted no publicity for himself, only the satisfaction of helping the best athletes. Steve Ovett had been helped already by him. He offered me £750 and, on 17 January, I was on my way to five weeks' midwinter training and competition in the warmth and sunshine of California.

First stop in Washington DC was not as I anticipated. The temperature was 25 degrees fahrenheit below freezing, and it was snowing. I have never known it so cold. But at least I was there. It was a dream come true, and everything was more incredible than I could have imagined.

The stadium in College Park, Maryland, in early January was packed with 18,000 people. That is more than can be accommodated in Britain's largest outdoor track arena at Crystal Palace. It dawned on me there and then why the American throwers perform so well in winter. The only time I had ever had that many people watching me, willing me on, was at the Olympics. The American athletes had it every other week in winter.

That night, I taught them a little lesson. I won. I only needed 65 feet 7 inches to do it but it was enough to beat the old enemy Feuerbach and give me a good start. Al and I flew together the next day to Los Angeles – from 25 degrees fahrenheit below to 75 degrees fahrenheit of heat.

We were heading for San Jose, a Californian community which had attracted most of the best American throwers in the mid-1970s.

At the airport I was met by Brian 'Crazy Horse' Oldfield, the world professional record holder. He had left the amateur sport in 1973 to earn some money on the Mike O'Hara ITA circuit. It had not been a great success, and four years later Oldfield, along with other ex-ITA men, was to be allowed back into the amateur world. But in early 1976 he was an outcast.

He was a startling sight in that airport lounge. All he wore was a pair of swimming trunks. 'How do you do,' he said mimicking an Oxford accent and leading me towards his sleek blue Cadillac.

Brian was only my chauffeur. My host was to be another world record holder, discus thrower John Powell. He happened to be a policeman, so we had that in common, but the San Jose Police Department must have paid its men more than they did in Cambridgeshire. John lived with Oldfield in a magnificent condominium with its own swimming pool and heated thermal bath. Outside was parked his new Porsche sports car with the number plate DISCUS I.

The training facilities they enjoyed there were fantastic. There was a physiotherapist constantly available, and every session was like an Olympic final . . . Feuerbach, Mac Wilkins, who was to win the Olympic discus gold medal that year, another 1976 Olympian, Pete Shmock, and three-time Olympian Marean Seidler, all training together with Powell and Oldfield in perfect weather and with the time to do it properly. Every training session attracted twenty to thirty spectators, so good was the competition. This continuous competitiveness of world-class throwers was very stimulating.

Of course, not all of these athletes were born in San Jose. Only Powell was a local. Feuerbach was an Iowa boy, Wilkins and Shmock from Oregon, and Seidler from New York. But they understood the advantages of a collective group of athletes exchanging ideas and know-

77

ledge, and giving each other a challenge in training. They had created their own post-university system – as a group of experts. In some ways we have tried to do that with the Southern Shot Squad without the same high standard and at weekends only (see page 134).

The first West Coast competition was the Sunkist meeting in Los Angeles. Naturally, we flew there. There was no second-class rail fare nonsense on the American indoor circuit. We were stars, and we were treated as such. Not that any of those spectators had heard of Geoff Capes before that Saturday. But they were to learn plenty that evening. I won. This unknown policeman from the backwoods of England had beaten the best in America. And he had done it with a new European, Commonwealth and British indoor record of 68 feet 10 inches.

The Los Angeles papers were full of it. They treat shot putting as a main event. Shot putters are as important to them as runners, and as big a draw for the promoters. The shot is given the full build-up by the announcers, and the journalists want to write about it. It was so different back home. Too many of the British writers know nothing of field events. Even a bad run in the 1500 metres is enough to keep anything about the shot out of their stories. Their only concern are races between 800 and 10,000 metres.

It is this sort of sports writing which leads to the ridiculous coverage Sebastian Coe had throughout 1980. He only had to cough to earn yards of newspaper comment. He is a super guy, and a great athlete. So is Steve Ovett. But they must feel embarrassed by the ridiculous extent of their media coverage. Pictures of girlfriends, stories about sisters' go-go dancing, chats with their mothers – we had the whole works. What we had too little of was informed writing about them as athletes.

In America I even made it into *Sports Illustrated*, the premier weekly sports magazine which devotes most of its space to baseball, basketball and American football, and almost none to foreigners. They wrote about my Los

Angeles performance and pictured me in colour. I began
to get the impression the American throwers were starting to resent my presence.

I went back to San Jose with them for another week's
training before the major meeting of my trip, the annual
event at the San Francisco Cow Palace. But disaster
struck. I tore a finger on my throwing hand. A doctor
and the physio patched me up, and they could not have
been more amazed than I was when I won that meeting
too, with 68 feet 5 inches. That was three out of three,
and there was another win to follow in Portland, Oregon,
with a putt of 68 feet ½ inch.

Finally, I was beaten. The finger was now far worse. I
had had the middle finger taped to the index finger to
give me enough support for the shot and, even though I
finished third in the second LA meeting, I managed a
putt of 67 feet 10½ inches. I lost again to Shmock the next
evening in my final meet in the United States, and then
headed north for Winnipeg in Canada. The temperature
was a complete contrast again – colder even than in
Washington – and I was soon nursing a cold as well as a
sore hand.

My training companion now was the top Canadian
Bruce Pirnie, an old friend and rival, and, when he took
me to watch a local major league ice hockey match, I was
introduced to the crowd of 20,000 as the Commonwealth
champion. It was more nerve-racking than throwing, but
it was all promotion for the Winnipeg Games we were to
compete it. That was my North American finale, and
what a climax! I putted 68 feet 10 inches, equalling the
European indoor record I had set in Los Angeles.

Five wins out of seven among the toughest shot putting
competition in the world – who could ask for a better
boost just six months before an Olympic Games?

I had only been home for a few days when I was off
again, this time to Munich for the European Indoor
Championships. I was weighing only 274 pounds now,
my lightest for years, and my torn finger was still painful.
I had had four cortisone injections along the tendon

79

sheath in an attempt to cure it, but I could still not throw without a strapping on my hand.

That caused an official inquiry in Munich. The international rules are blunt about strapping: 'No device of any kind – e.g. the taping of two or more fingers together – which in any way assists the competitor when making a throw, shall be allowed.'

The only exception is for an open cut or wound, but tape on the wrist is permitted with the approval of the official meeting doctor. That permission I had – the first time I had ever needed it in competition – but it was the finger tape which upset the officials.

As usual with a small party, Britain had not brought a team doctor, but the Polish team doctor hand-made a finger stall which protected my injury without offering it any support. You can imagine my mood – not a pleasant one after arguing with officials for two hours.

I could not risk another pain-killing injection because the cortisone used was steroid-based. The pain was bearable initially, but I was not going to lose this event after the confidence the US trip had given me. Everything had to go right, and it did. The Russian Barishnikov even helped unwittingly in the warm-up when he looked at my covered finger and taped wrist and sneered. That made me madder than ever.

I went into the circle for the first time and blasted out 67 feet $\frac{1}{4}$ inch. I felt I had to go hell for leather in case the finger went, and that first throw was the end of true competition. Barishnikov and the East German Gerd Lochmann could not put it together in reply.

In the second round I reached 66 feet 8 inches which also beat anything the others were to achieve in the entire competition; I fouled on my third round, threw 66 feet 3 inches on my fourth and then made certain of the gold medal with 67 feet $8\frac{3}{4}$ inches in the fifth. The best Barishnikov came out with, using his discus-style rotational technique, was 65 feet $8\frac{1}{4}$ inches in the first round, and that was only good enough for the bronze behind Lochmann's first-round throw of 66 feet 7 inches.

Even the news that evening that the American Terry
Albirtton had reached a world-record distance of 71 feet
$8\frac{1}{2}$ inches in Hawaii that weekend could not spoil my
delight. I was on target for the Olympics.

I hibernated for the next eight weeks. Stuart and I had
decided to start the season later than others and to avoid
wasting too much energy on unnecessary competitions.
The Olympics were coming, and nothing else mattered.
The hours of sweat I was spending in the weights room
and the shot circle were not fun. In training you hurt,
and I had no intention of hurting just for a garden fête.
In 1976 it was the Olympics alone that counted and
everything else, however important to others, was a dis-
traction.

I even refused the British Board's invitation to compete for Britain against East Germany; whoever heard of
an international match against such a strong nation on
1 May! The weakness of British shot putting was really
exposed that day – we had to put out discus thrower Bill
Tancred, and neither he nor Bob Dale made 60 feet.

My first competition was a week later at Grangemouth – a men's invitation shot during the women's
international match against the Netherlands. What a
start! I threw 21.18 metres (69 feet 6 inches), the best in
the world at that early stage of the season, and the
second best of my career. It was so easy, too. The best
always are, but in Olympic year it was a tremendous
boost.

Next I took on the Russians in an international match
in Kiev. I am not a lover of the Soviet Union as a place.
It depresses me. For such a wealthy country everything
appears so poor and second rate. But I had a great
contest with Barishnikov: my 69 feet $4\frac{3}{4}$ inches to his 69
feet 11 inches – my best came in the third round, his with
his rotational technique in the fourth.

Those throws ranked as the best and the third best in
the world that year – and the second best was mine at
Grangemouth. The two best throwers in the world had
met just a few weeks before the Olympics and were

81

throwing superbly. But do you think we warranted a decent mention in the British press? They were too busy writing about our women sprinters who had been blown to good times by a howling gale.

My consistency continued throughout May. Four days after the Kiev match, I threw 68 feet 8¾ inches to beat the Finn Stahlberg by nearly 5 feet at Crystal Palace, and then two days later I travelled to Gateshead for the Superspike Classic, an event held to raise money for the International Athletes Club – it was a fantastic success despite bad weather.

Around 10,000 Geordies turned up on a cold, windy evening, largely, I suspect, to cheer their great hero, Brendan Foster. Unfortunately, Big Bren tripped and fell with only about 200 yards left of the mile, but I gave them plenty to cheer for. The other performances may have been ruined by the weather, but I had a trick up my sleeve to beat the cold – a bucket of hot water.

The rain fell as we were competing, but all the time I kept my shot in the hot water. When it was my turn to throw, I was ready with a hot shot and warm fingers. It worked, too. I threw a season's best of 69 feet 6¾ inches in the fifth round, and with my final putt set a new Commonwealth record of 70 feet 8½ inches. Just one more foot to the world record, I was thinking that night.

I had one more competition before the Olympic trials – helping out East Midlands in the Inter-Counties Championships at Crystal Palace – but it was a walkover as usual. I won by nearly 8 feet, beating Bob Dale, a 6 foot 6 inch thrower from Stoke whom I was coaching myself. He was the closest to me again in the Olympic trials because Winch was missing, but this time there was only 7 feet difference because Bob managed to get over 62 feet, a personal best and very good for someone who only took up the shot when he was twenty-three.

The police gave me three weeks off before I left for the Olympics, and for two of them I lived with Stuart at his home in Ware. I had one more competition, against the Poles and Canadians at Crystal Palace, winning this time by almost 8 feet. Then I set sail for Canada. Yes, set sail. I had chosen to cross the Atlantic by ship to avoid the trauma of flying.

The British Board had arranged for me to sail on the Polish ship, the *Stefan Battary*, and the ship's gymnasium had been equipped with the necessary weights for me. Eight days before the rest of Britain's team flew out of Heathrow, I was sailing out of Tilbury.

I even found my own masseur among the passengers – a Newmarket veterinary surgeon who did his best to cope with the conditions of the human body. The ship's captain ordered the gym closed to all but me for two hours each day, and everything looked wonderful.

There were problems, however. One was seasickness. The other was a mid-Atlantic storm which had the weights sliding along the smooth gym floor. Lifting here required a technique never before used by the world's weightlifters. I would wait for the bar to roll along the gym floor towards me, lift it in one movement and then for the next lift I would have to wait while it made its way back along the gym floor with the next pitch of the ship.

I enjoyed the eight-day voyage. It was an experience. I saw icebergs and whales, and we travelled down the St Lawrence Seaway to Montreal through some beautiful scenery. But I would not recommend it as a way to prepare for an Olympic Games.

In those eight days I lost some of my edge. The environment was unnatural and, more important, I was unable to throw for a crucial period before the Games. It was my own fault for choosing that manner of transport and, although I cannot use it as an excuse for what was to follow, the sea trip contributed something to my downfall – of that I'm sure.

The Olympic Village was like something out of Ancient Egypt – a strange and wonderful collection of pyramid buildings that were to be my home for the next three weeks. I arrived the day before the official party, but there was no special medal for being first on that occasion. I had to share like everybody else and, in the cramped British quarters, that meant four to a room only 4 yards by 7. My three room-mates were Peter Tancred, Chris Black and Paul Dickenson, the smallest of them 6 feet tall and the lightest $16\frac{1}{2}$ stone. The crush can easily be imagined and, with all of us incapable of fending for ourselves, the mess of used clothing soon threatened to have the entire place condemned as unfit for human habitation.

Village life can be boring. It is the routine, the monotony, which affects you. There should be plenty to do, good training facilities, entertainment and certainly enough people to talk with. But you are there for one purpose and, since all your thoughts are addressed to one particular moment, time hangs on your hands.

It is not surprising that fit, strong young men and women occasionally let their hair down. It is only surprising in this enlightened age that officials still react like Victorian schoolteachers to any high jinks. And there are always plenty of them. In Montreal, the throwers hid the canoeists' beds after the canoeists had bad-mouthed us about the time they claimed we were spending on the physio's couch.

The claustrophobic conditions were hardly conducive to good preparation for competition. British officials were just not on top of their job. They had been duped into accepting poor accommodation – some men were even sharing five to a room – and yet were upset when the more well established athletes made their own arrangements to escape.

The BBC came to the rescue for some of us. Alan Pascoe moved into a spare room they had, and I moved out to share with Stuart at one of the best hotels in town, where he was staying as part of the television commentary team. At least it was quieter and more comfortable, and I was asleep before 10.30 on the night before the qualifying competition.

The last thing you need at that stage is to bump into your opponents, meet them eye-to-eye, perhaps in the village dining room. There is so much psyching going on at that time that you do not want the confrontations caused by claims like 'I'm bigger than you, look at me' – which may happen even when you are just standing next to a rival in a queue.

I kept thinking of a Bruce Lee film I had seen about kung-fu champions being shipped to an island to fight to the death, and the way in which they looked at each other on the voyage to the island. It was reminiscent of an Olympic village.

The pressure is unbelievable. You need to be away from it to prepare properly. I know they say that meeting in the village, the gathering of all sports and all nationalities is what the Olympics is about, but, if your mind is set on winning, it is the last thing you want.

At some events, Stuart and I have had a few beers, at others gone to the cinemas, but that evening I put myself to sleep on a diet of TV cowboy films in Stuart's hotel room. I was up again at 6.30 but I had slept well. You need to. Once you are awake, you are a nervous wreck. At least I am. I cannot think straight. I reckon the nearest equivalent must be a woman close to childbirth. You do strange things, out of character.

I had eliminated as much of the stress as possible – the room-mates coming in and out of the room, the late-nighters who never think of others when they crash back from the disco, the girls who hang around, the card schools. But you cannot eliminate your thoughts, and mine were always all over the place.

The pre-competition formalities are not helpful. They have to be precise and rigid, but they increase the pressure and the feeling that you are going into something unnatural. You are nervous, but on the warm-up track you can see that others are as nervous and that helps.

You jog, bound, throw a little, just to settle into a more normal routine. Wilf Paish, the national coach, came out to the warm-up area to help me that day. But, when the loudspeaker calls the contestants together with the command 'shot putters', you are on your own. Everybody

85

stops and you file, elephant-fashion, into the unwelcoming stadium.

It was about 10.15 in the morning, a most unnatural time of the day to be competing. There were not too many spectators but there was a sense of occasion, even for this qualifying competition. The contestants feel like gladiators, emerging into the sunlight of the open arena, parading in a single file to shot area.

We were allowed two warm-up throws. I had been drawn to go into the circle fifth for the real thing. The qualifying standard was 19.40 metres – an easy distance but so far away when you are tense. You can leave as soon as you have achieved it but you have only three attempts.

I made it comfortably with a first throw of 20.40 metres, but qualifying was not such a formality for others. George Woods, the silver medallist from Munich, only made it as the twelfth qualifier, 5 centimetres short of the required distance.

The Olympic Games seem to have a special effect on throwers. They slow us down. You do not feel as if it is the usual you out there. The legs belong to another person. How else can you explain why, on the most important day in their lives, people fail so completely? So-called experts say it is because we have to come off the drugs. That is ridiculous. It attacks different people on different days.

In Montreal, Woods only made it as a lucky loser; in Munich he had won a silver medal. Reichenbach failed to make the final in Montreal but he had won a European silver medal. Stahlberg had thrown well over 21 metres but only qualified with 19.40 metres, the exact distance necessary. It was unusually hot – officially 31 degrees centigrade – and even warmer on the airless floor of the arena. Perhaps that left people feeling limp.

I went back quickly to Stuart's hotel, showered and felt good. I had qualified with one throw, the effort expended had been minimal and I had only to occupy another twenty-four hours before the main event. That evening I had a meal in a city steak bar and was put to sleep by watching endless repeats of Olympic heats on the television in our room. But not for long. I woke at all hours of that night.

I had breakfast at about 8.30 and reported back to the village by 10.00. Another three-hour sleep, and then the long walk to the warm-up stadium. That was the worst part. My mind was so full of thoughts, about the family, friends, the police, sponsors, coach, colleagues . . . what were they thinking, doing, saying? The hardest part was thinking of a shot competition. Wilf Paish walked with me and Stuart was there when we arrived, but I felt lonely, apart from them.

Again came those dreaded words, 'shot putters'. We gathered in a group, the twelve of us, looking at each other to see how ready each was. In the holding pen, we checked in . . . Feuerbach, Woods, Shmock, Beyer, Barishnikov, Mironov, Gies, Hoglund, Rothenburg, Brabec, Stahlberg – the greatest names in shot putting, every one of us had thrown over 20.50 metres in our time and several of us over 21 metres and 70 feet. But this was the Olympics; anybody could win it. There could never be a favourite. All chances were equal.

For twenty minutes we sat there. Nobody spoke. The Eastern Europeans were stone-faced, unsmiling, expressionless. We avoided each others' eyes. Time dragged. We tried to think of the details, what we had been told, what we had learnt. It was warm and close but we kept our tracksuits on. Christ, the strain was unbelievable. How much nervous energy must we have used up in those twenty minutes? It seemed like a lifetime.

Finally, you are out in the arena. It is hot, and you are throwing on the sunny side. There is a crowd of 70,000 for this second day of the Olympic Games, and there cannot be many who are not rooting for the three Americans. Feuerbach is their hero. I jog around, stretching, checking every muscle. All are working. I take a warm-up throw. It flies, over 21 metres, perhaps beyond the Olympic record marker. Things are good. I have made five throws over 21 metres consecutively in my final practice session the day before qualifying. The sensation is still there. I can feel it.

I sit down to wait my turn. Ten minutes pass. I begin to feel cold, to tighten. I get up, run a little, bound, stretch, anything to get my looseness back. The competition is under way. My name is called. First throw: 20.15 metres. I'm lying fourth after the first round, behind Barishnikov, Beyer and Hoglund. Feuerbach has not even made 20 metres. It could be worse for me.

Next round a small improvement to 20.21 metres. Feuerbach has taken the lead now with 20.55. In the third round, another improvement to 20.36, edging up, but Barishnikov is back in front with the first 21 metre throw of the competition and I am back in sixth place. At least I have three more throws.

The fourth round is a few centimetres worse – 20.32 metres – and the fifth just 20.31. I am being consistent, but where is that big one? Now Beyer unleashes his best throw to date – 21.05 metres. I have one last chance.

The throw is good. Estimates put it at near 21 metres, good enough for third or fourth place. But then disaster strikes. It is judged a foul. I have blown the big chance.

How do you explain it? Beyer's winner would have been good enough only for fifth in Munich. Barishnikov, who had set a world record of 22 metres just fifteen days earlier, could throw only 21 metres on that day. Feuerbach was 2 feet behind his best for the season. It is a crazy event, shot putting, and never as crazy as at the Olympics.

And me? How could I explain being a metre behind what I had done in training the same week? Stuart believes it was technical. I was 'blocking out', putting my left foot in the stopboard at the wrong place and restricting my hip drive. But, to be honest, it was all in the mind. I froze. I threw a reasonable series but my mind would not release my body for the big throw. I was not loose.

The effect of failure was devastating. I wanted to be

away from the stadium as soon as possible. A few British pressmen wanted explanations. I couldn't help them. I didn't know myself. Some guy rubbed it in by asking who had won the shot, without knowing I had hoped it would be me. I gave away to a little boy a little Union Jack I'd been carrying in my kit bag. What the hell would everybody I cared about be thinking now? My family at home, my sister Christine whom I had not seen for twelve years and who had travelled from Boston in Massachusetts to watch me?

Capes did not go back to the village; instead he went to Stuart Storey's room at the Constellation Hotel. Ron Pickering was with Stuart when Capes arrived. Little was said, little needed to be said. Ron made his excuses and left. 'If you need me, just holler,' were his parting words to Storey.

'The moment Ron left, Geoff broke down. All he could say was that he could have won it. For an hour and a half he cried, a lot of the time on me,' recalls Storey.

'Finally, I told him to take a shower. I went next door and borrowed a bottle of Scotch from Ron. When I took it to Geoff he was sitting in the bath, fully clothed, with the shower full on. I left him there. When he came out, the bottle was empty. And then he was okay.'

There are times when drink helps. A good cry did me a power of good that day, too. I can recommend it when you are low. I can't remember now whom I was feeling most sorry for – the others who had helped me so willingly or myself. I did not see much more of those Olympics, nor did I want to. It was not the happiest for me or for Britain – just one bronze medal for the athletes. I found a quiet cabin up on a lonely lake and went fishing for a week.

I returned to Britain with the rest of the British team to be met by my family. For two days I did little but sleep, but during the next three weeks I was to win three events: the Coca-Cola International, the AAA Championship and the Gateshead Games. Each time I threw further than I had in Montreal, and in Gateshead I beat Shmock and Feuerbach with a throw of 21.20 metres, enough to have won in Montreal.

But what did it matter? What did it mean? On the one day in four years it had mattered. I had won nothing. Shot putting was becoming a penance, not a pleasure. My heart went out of it that winter. I won another European indoor silver in 1977, and a bronze in 1978, but I was free-wheeling. I had dedicated myself for four years, no, more like ten years, to that day in Montreal, and it had brought me nothing but misery. I needed rest and relaxation, I wanted to enjoy life. It would be three years before I took shot putting seriously again.

11

A Lot of Old Junk

When Arthur Gold was secretary of the British Amateur Athletic Board he suggested that, to eliminate drug-taking in athletics, shot putting should be abolished. That was nearly ten years ago — before the first recognized drug tests in athletics.

The tests proved him wrong. Shot putting was not the exception but the rule as far as drug taking was concerned. Sport as a whole was riddled with competitors taking drugs to improve their performances in training and competition. Of twenty-one athletes found guilty since the tests for anabolic steroids were introduced about six years ago, only four have been shot putters. Just as many have been runners, and more than half have been women. Most significantly, all but six of those caught have been from Eastern European countries.

Geoff Capes has been dope-tested on twenty-four occasions since the tests became official International Amateur Athletic Federation policy in 1975. Not once has he given a positive sample.

Anabolic steroids? They are old hat. They passed their peak in 1975 when the tests were introduced. Throwers just laugh at the tests now. They and their coaches know more about steroids than all the testers in the world. The laboratories are years behind us.

Not that it is only throwers who take artificial aids to improve performance. Ninety per cent of top athletes have taken one kind of artificial aid or another during their careers. Just look at those who have been caught in athletics alone: throwers, jumpers, hurdlers, middle-

91

distance runners. That only leaves sprinters, and nobody can tell me that they are clean.

There has not been a wholly clean world drugs record in athletics since 1960. And athletes do not only take steroids – I have seen them taking amphetamines. I have seen them taking hash and coke (cocaine). I have seen vitamin B injected. I have seen them recently taking substances even I don't recognize. And it was not only throwers who were taking them.

I have had girls in Britain coming up to me asking what they should take and where they can get it – girls who are runners and girls who are not even out of their teens. I have talked with top people in other sports, and they know as much about drug-taking as I do. The testers have even caught competitors in swimming, weightlifting, rowing and cycling events. Hardly one Olympic sport is not involved.

I remember when Jeff Teale retired in about 1971 he told a national newspaper that he had taken anabolic steroids. He said he had taken half a tablet a day. The world's throwers fell about laughing. It was like saying he had drunk two bottles of milk for all the effect it could have had on him. But that was what it was like in the late 1960s and early 1970s. Everybody was experimenting. It was all trial and error.

The dangers have been shouted from the rooftops. We have been threatened with hair loss, impotency, cancer, just about everything imaginable. But steroids are like aspirins. Take two and you cure a headache, take the bottle and they will kill you. You have to be sensible and seek advice.

Steroids are not addictive. Amphetamines, the suppressants, the uppers and downers, the cocaine and morphine, those are the real dangers in sport. They improve performances and, because of their addictive quality, are deadly. I've seen an athlete during an actual competition put a towel over his leg to prevent officials seeing him sticking a needle into it. And he was sitting right next to the throwing circle!

Most of the anabolic steroids are, of course, taken orally. When Ilona Slupianek, the East German who won the 1978 European gold medal and the 1980 Olympic title, was convicted, we were told it was because her doctor did not use a long enough needle. He had injected the drug into the body fat instead of the muscle and it had been retained in her body for longer than it should have been. So the usual clearance period of two to four weeks was not enough, and she was caught. And that is the only way the testers catch anybody – when the athletes make a mistake.

The dope tests are a joke. For one thing, there are athletes taking substances which cannot be tested. Testosterone is the best known of them. It is a natural body hormone, and therefore the tests cannot determine whether its presence is natural or artificial.

Now athletes come off the steroids a month ahead of competition, but they take testosterone as a substitute. It has the same effect. A woman can even produce the same effect perfectly legally – by taking pills similar to contraceptives. But they are not the ones you get from the family planning clinic. These ones are controlled and made up specially, and they simply make her more like a man.

But in the first place we had to find out what drugs were being taken in other countries and what effect they had. We were desperate for information. On one occasion we went around the rooms of foreign athletes staying at the Crystal Palace hostel, taking any powders and tablets we found, and even syringes, to send for analysis. That taught us a great deal. But most of the information gradually fed through to us on the grapevine.

So what are the drugs and what do they do? The most commonly used branded anabolic steroid drugs in Britain are the well-known Dianabol – the one everybody calls Big D – and Stromba, which are both taken orally, and Deccadurablin, which is the injectable drug and lasts longer in the body than the oral variety. None of them will enable someone to throw a 16 pound shot 70 feet. They are not magic. All drugs do is assist in training. Their intended medical purpose is to stimulate muscle and bone growth, and they are useful for old people. My mother is matron of an old people's home, and she has the responsibility for giving them to many of her patients.

With a fit athlete, their most important effect is the stimulation of competitiveness and aggression. An athlete taking them will be able to train harder, longer and more often; the drug may not even be responsible for producing extra bulk and strength, but it can give an athlete the capacity to produce these qualities by enabling him to do extra training.

In Britain, you can get hold of these drugs from a friendly doctor but, if you are abroad, you will not need even a prescription. I have seen them on sale over the counter in France. At the European Indoor Championships in San Sebastian in Spain, I saw a packet of fifty capsules in the cupboard of the hotel physiotherapist. In sports like powerlifting and body building, they are accepted, and few doctors are going to get upset about administering them. There are far greater menaces in the world. Drink for one.

We cannot blame the Eastern Europeans for the prevalence of drug taking. It started in the United States. No doubt about that. None of their athletes has yet been caught because they have so few tests there. But they began it long before I came into the sport at the top level. One just kept looking at the Americans and wondering. How were they producing performances which were so superior? What did they have?

Every thrower can remember the 1960s. There was a surge of brilliant performances by Americans. In one year the shot record went up $2\frac{1}{2}$ feet. In five years it improved by more than 7 feet. And it was not a soft record to start with. Parry O'Brien, a great thrower, had set it. Drugs had to be a major factor in the improvement. But which drugs? We had to compete, but we were in the dark.

94

Now, of course, we have easy references telling us what to take, how to take it and when to take it. I have Bill Pearl's book on training methods, published in this country and one of the most authoritative manuals available. It has an entire chapter on the taking of anabolic steroids. Weight-training and body-building magazines in Britain openly talk of it, and give their readers information on how to obtain supplies. Any lay person needing precise information on amounts to take need only consult one of the medical profession's reference books. That will give the exact dosage necessary and advisable.

Of course, anybody who takes drugs without medical advice is stupid. They don't need testing for drugs; they need their heads examining. But advice is available. You have to be secretive about it, but it is there. Doctors, coaches, even some officials, will help. It doesn't mean they approve of drug-taking, but they know that, without drugs, athletes cannot compete on equal terms, so they are prepared to set aside their professional judgements.

I pulled out of the Coca-Cola Invitation meeting in 1976 when it became the first invitation meeting where dope tests were used. All the throwers did. It was a protest against the victimization of throwers. In those days we were always the targets. But it was also a protest at the complexity of the drug rules.

One Canadian girl athlete was banned when she was found to have taken, quite unknowingly, a banned drug. It turned out that the drug was contained in a cold-cure tablet available over the counter in any chemist.

When we said we did not know what drugs were banned, officials told us to buy a copy of the rulebook. But that is so complex nobody can understand it. It bans drugs by groups, not by name or, even better, by brand. How do we laymen know what not to take? At one time I was scared I might be taking something as simple as aspirin which might be banned.

The tests are not perfect anyway. I have a friend who arrived at a meeting not expecting tests, and could not avoid having to take one. He knew it would be positive. So he persuaded a tester to pee in the bottle for him.

At the Commonwealth Games in Canada, one of the athletes' wives was working in the testing centre. Word soon got about that the Canadians were laughing. Samples were tipped down the sink and one of the testers was a supplier of Dianabol to Canadian athletes.

I have seen a person taking another competitor's place in the dope test. It can easily happen because the testers never check on identity, particularly in the lower key domestic meetings.

All the tester knows are the names of those who have to be tested. Often he will not recognize them from Adam. He just comes up to you, asks if your name is Brown and takes your word for it.

Once, when a British team went to East Germany, there was to be dope testing, but the East Germans did not have the laboratory to analyse the samples. So we were to bring them back to London with us. I was asked to carry them through customs at the German end, and they were then loaded in the hold of the plane. Surprise, surprise, when we came to collect them at Heathrow, we found all the samples broken!

The tests are not legal in any case. None would stand up in a court of law. As a policeman, I frequently objected to them in the early days, but it got me nowhere. A motorist tested by police for alcohol in the blood must be given a sample for his own analysis. The officials refuse to do this in athletics. They split the sample into two but keep both halves for themselves and do not allow you any check on their results.

Athletes use various substances to 'wash out' the evidence from their bodies before they report for testing. These are called diuretics; when drunk, they cause the excretion of fluid from the body. When athletes say they 'waste' themselves before a dope test, that is what they mean.

At the Olympic Games in Moscow, athletes were taking diuretics wherever you looked. The shot putt winner

1967 – primitive early training facilities at Carter's Park in Holbeach: a borrowed concrete cricket strip, a home-made stop board and a rock to hold it in place. Stuart Storey was already my coach

This would shake the East Germans – weight-training in Holbeach Youth Club; a piano and a convenient wall serve as weight supports

An early appearance, *circa* 1968, for the AAAs in their annual match against Loughborough Past and Present

Perhaps one of these will do for lunch

A day's food in 1976

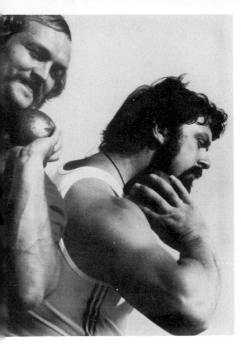

Back to back, and shots from twelve paces – the competition with Al Feuerbach in 1974 had all the appearances of a Western duel

The old enemy – Jeff Teale – 'always reminded me of Desperate Dan in the comics'

Mike Winch – 'the only thrower in Britain who has given me any serious competition since 1971'

Udo Beyer – 1976 Olympic champion competing here at the 1978 European Championships

Modern British training facilities? Outdoors in midwinter, snow on the ground.
At least the tennis crowd have stayed indoors

Winning a bronze medal in Rome, 1974, at the European Championships

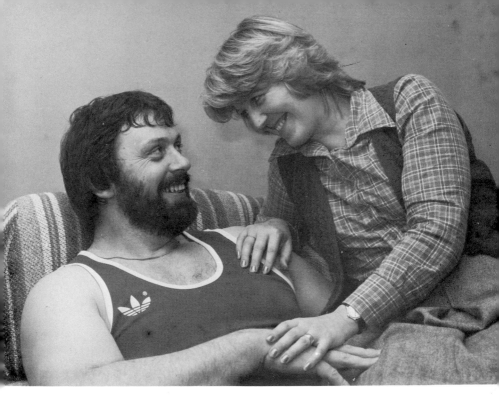

Happy families – at home with wife Gillian . . .

. . . a ride for daughter Emma . . .

. . . and Lewis, when only four,
following in father's footsteps

Carrying the flag for Britain at the 1978 European Championships in Prague – a few days later I was disqualified and sent home

Three of a kind – with the other shot medallists at the 1978 Commonwealth Games in Edmonton – Bruno Pauletto (*left*) and Bishop Dolegiewicz, both Canadians

Vladimir Kiselov, 1980 Olympic champion

Aleksandr Baryshnikov, a 22 metre thrower but only good enough for silver at the 1980 Olympics

A *Daily Mail* cartoon during the Olympic boycott controversy – guess who is the only identifiable athlete?

'The Russians don't want us in Moscow till our troops are pulled out of Espiritu Santo.'

I can't resist a challenge – here I beat all-comers over 20 stone in a 400 metres race. I won by more than 100 metres. The beer was my prize

Believe it or not, I'm standing in for Olympic champion David Wilkie at this sponsored swim

Feathered friend – one of the many birds I have bred in my back garden for showing in competitions

Pedal power – competing in a BBC TV Superstars event

Champions all – appearing for the Sports Aid Foundation. *Left to right:* Chris Baillieu (*rowing*), Keith Remfry (*judo*), Robin Cousins (*skating*), myself, Reg White (*sailing*) and David Wilkie (*swimming*)

The short-shift, long-base technique, favoured by the East Germans and
myself. Note how the left arm keeps its original position until the left leg hits
the ground, retaining the vital 'torque' which provides so much of the thrust

Weight-training in 1980

Kiselov was drinking from a bottle containing a white substance which resembled liquid paraffin. I had never seen that before and I could only guess what affect it had.

Before the competition, I had seen both Russians, Kiselov and Barishnikov, being taken away from the other throwers into a small room. I asked the British coach Wilf Paish to follow them. When he did, a doctor coming from the room pushed him out of the way. He had a syringe in his hand. Okay, so we can only guess, but it makes you wonder.

One of the other throwers in Moscow was told he had to present himself for testing. They had chosen the first four places and the sixth place. I was fifth. When he heard, he took this packet of powder from his bag, mixed it with a drink and swallowed it. When he saw me watching, he just winked.

Drug-takers are not so blatant as they used to be. It wouldn't happen now, but I found a syringe in a changing room once and I knew who had been there ahead of me. Then there was the famous case of the Czech world-record holder who came to Edinburgh for a meeting and actually asked a senior British official to direct her to the nearest chemist. She showed him a prescription she had. It was for anabolic steroids. He wanted to make a case of it, but was persuaded it would be only his word against hers.

So what do I think of drug-taking? Athletes at present have three choices. They can take part in club athletics and never aspire to anything greater. They can become international athletes without any chance of succeeding in major events. Or they can choose to take what others take and stand a chance of beating them. It is the athletes' own decision. Nobody else can make it for them.

Is there any reason why they shouldn't take them? Medically, I don't think the case against them has been proved. If these particular drugs are taken under proper medical direction, I do not believe the danger to health is greater than that presented by other prescribed drugs.

The moral argument only stands up if the drugs are

available to an exclusive group and the competition is unfair. But that isn't so.

The real danger, in my opinion, lies in the stupid belief that, if a drug increases training capacity, a greater quantity of the drug will increase it further. That way lies disaster.

Unfortunately, the present rules are not a deterrent to drug-taking. Officials devise them, make elaborate tests to enforce them and then, for political reasons, let the guilty off with a slapped wrist. What sort of deterrent was it that let three women runners back into the Olympics only ten months after they had been caught by a test?

What I would prefer is an amnesty. Let's start afresh. Let us say that all the old records will be ruled out. The IAAF will fix a date on which records will start again from scratch for the next generation. After that date, anybody found guilty will be banned for life – a mandatory sentence – and meanwhile the IAAF will introduce an educational programme to advise youngsters on ways of improving training and performance other than using drugs.

I'll start such a programme with the group of promising youngsters I coach. I will never tell any of them to take drugs. I am determined that they will never need to take drugs. Indeed, I will tell them not to take drugs. And, perhaps because it is me telling them, because it is somebody who has been part of the drug generation, they will take notice.

My advice to them will be to give up the sport before they take drugs. It's not worth it. It has gone too far. I have been in the sport during its worst days. If the new generation has to beat the old standards, the old records, of course they are going to have to take drugs. There is no way anybody can reach beyond those levels without them. The present generation's performances will never be exceeded naturally.

What we must do is clear the way for the young. Do away with the records just as they have ruled out wind-assisted or hand-timed performances. Rub out all that has gone before, and let the new generation set their own standards. Of course, they will be lower. But, if all of them are aiming at the new standards, that will not concern them.

12

The Bounced Czech

The *Times correspondent called it an 'incident'. Other, more popular, papers named it flippantly 'the case of the bounced Czech'. Whatever the title, the story had an unhappy ending: at the 1978 European Championships in Prague, Geoff Capes became the first British athlete in living memory to be disqualified before even entering the stadium.*

The trouble had begun almost certainly a fortnight previously, 4000 miles away, in Edmonton, Canada. Capes had won a mediocre shot competition at the Commonwealth Games with a throw of 19.77 metres (64 feet 10½ inches), and had threatened at the winners' press conference to withdraw from the Prague event. It would be, he said, a waste of time competing against Communist-bloc competitors who had been 'scientifically prepared by the use of steroids'.

On Capes's arrival in Prague, the local newspapers took up the charge. An official government paper described Capes as 'a vehicle of the capitalist press out to blacken the name of Communist athletes'. He was, it said, voicing his opinion only to satisfy the press.

I heard about what the local papers were saying from the team interpreter, a woman. She read it out to a group of us sitting in the stands watching earlier competitions. We all had a good laugh, and thought no more about it. The only thing on our minds in Prague was the weather. It was appalling – cold, wet and windy.

Two days later, the day before the final, I warmed up

for the qualifying round with the British hammer thrower Chris Black helping me. I was wearing numbers on my tracksuit, on the kit bag I would be taking into the arena and on the back of my vest. There was no number on the front of my vest.

After my warm-up I went to the official desk to report for competition. My numbers were checked – vest, bag, tracksuit, okay, off you go – and out I went to qualify with 20.08 metres and then straight back to the village. No problems, no hassle, everything as it should be.

Next day, the same thing – same warm-up, same numbers, same procedures. We marched in – same official at the desk. I was feeling marvellous, well warmed up, positive, raring to go, the best mood of my life. I'd won a bronze in the 1974 Europeans, and this was going to be better. I was hyped up as never before.

I couldn't stop moving around; I was on edge as you can be when the adrenalin starts building up. My turn in the queue. It was the same official as yesterday. 'Numbers check. Vest, front. Where's your number on your front?'

'I've left it in my room in the village. You checked me yesterday, said it was okay.'

He looked blank, as though I was nothing to him. 'That was yesterday, not today.'

'Now, look here,' I said, 'don't get me mad. There's five minutes to go to the competition. I haven't another number with me; it's a mile away in the village.'

'No number, no competition.' He said it without a trace of emotion. You could hardly see his lips move. I offered to take the number off my tracksuit. 'Can't do that,' he said.

'So how am I going to compete?' I asked. I was getting desperate, beginning to panic.

'No competition,' he said.

That did it. 'I'll sort it out when I get out there,' I said angrily.

Then came the shout to walk out to the arena. I joined

the line-up. The numbers official tried to stop me. Two other officials joined him, and then a security guard. Two took hold of me, and started pulling and tugging me away from the line-up.

I was really boiling now. I swore at them and yanked my arms away suddenly. One official fell on the floor and slid away on his backside. I moved quickly to catch up with the other throwers. I was through the door and up the steps before two more men jumped on me.

I gave them a push. Both bounced off the walls of the narrow corridor. I was past them, and with my fellow competitors. I sat down with them. A few seconds went by but obviously a commotion was going on in the background. The numbers official had called the International Amateur Athletic Federation technical official, Joseph Sirs, a Hungarian.

Sirs knew me. We had met often enough around Europe. He asked me what the problem was. I told him my story.

'Why did you do it?' he asked.

'Because a bloody man got hold of me and pulled me. What do you expect me to do?'

Sirs did not have an answer. 'It was ungentlemanly,' he said. 'We can't have it.'

Marea Hartman, one of the British officials, was fetched. I told her my story. Then I had to explain it to the British men's team chief, Bob Stinson, who was secretary of the British Amateur Athletic Board.

By now, Sirs had had a meeting with other officials, just a few yards from where I sat. All were from Eastern European countries.

'You're suspended,' said Sirs.

I couldn't believe it. 'You can't do that,' I said, and Stinson backed me on that point. They said they had done it. No apology was asked for or offered.

The other throwers had been warming up in the stadium, but they had been called off the field and the event delayed while the so-called jury of appeal met. Nothing changed. I was disqualified for 'serious misconduct and unsporting behaviour towards officials in the call room.'

Udo Beyer, the East German Olympic champion and world-record holder, came up to ask me what was happening. When I told him, he said he was sorry. 'I'd have done the same,' he said.

Later the numbers official came to apologize and shake my hand. 'I didn't want this to happen,' he said. 'It wasn't that serious.'

But I was out. The European Athletic Association secretary, Pierre Dasriaux, had the cheek to say that since I was a policeman I should know how to behave. At no time did the IAAF, the European AA or the British Board ask for my version of events. Stinson, my own manager, said my behaviour was 'inexcusable'. The British officials could not wait to get me out of Prague. In their minds, officials are always right. I might have had more chance had I been a runner. But a thrower, and Geoff Capes to boot, was too good an opportunity.

It did not stop when I was back in England. I came back two days before the rest of the team. My chief constable was fantastic about it. He was the only one who took my word for what happened. But the British Board took only the word of the Czech. It was typical of their pussy-footing attitude to all important decisions.

I was called to a meeting in London with the chairman of the Board, Arthur McAllister. Even then they did not accept my version. None of them had been present in that call room but they had accepted without question the word of the official. It was officials against athletes. They had not given me backing at any stage, and here they were telling me that it was all my fault.

Chris Brasher, who was disqualified himself at the 1956 Olympic Games but later reinstated, asked all the right questions in the *Observer* right after the incident. Why did the Czech official not point the problem out to the referee, who could have asked me to unpin the number from my tracksuit? Why didn't Bob Stinson take me to the jury of appeal to explain my side of the argument and perhaps apologize there and then? I apologized later to the Czech official and there were no hard feelings between us.

Even the reprimand was not sufficient punishment to satisfy some of the Board members. They wanted my blood. Six months later, there was enormous opposition within the Board to my selection for the European Indoor Championships in Vienna.

Certain officials whose responsibilities and ambitions lay in international affairs felt it would embarrass them for me to be allowed to compete in Europe again so soon. Fortunately, the Board had a new secretary, David Shaw, a professional who wasn't part of the old clique. He stood up and said I must go. I went and I won the silver medal – my sixth medal for Britain in those championships on the occasion of my sixtieth appearance for my country.

Shaw apart, Britain's senior officials had confirmed every view I had on their contribution to British athletics. There are hundreds of them at club level who do a fantastic job for little return beyond a vote of thanks at the annual dinner and the satisfaction of putting something back into a sport they probably enjoyed when they were young. But there are too many who want a better return on their time. They want power, they want glory, and they want trips. And, if the athletes get in their way, they are kicked aside.

13

Three Steps Backwards

Athletes anticipate post-Olympic anti-climax. The year which follows the Olympics has traditionally been one in which the international-class athlete will set his sights lower, and free-wheel and relax before working himself up for the end of the next two-year cycle.

Capes had enjoyed four successful years, and could look back even from the disappointment of Montreal to consistent annual progress in his event. But was there incentive to improve further? It was to be a long time before Capes found it. For the first time in his life in 1977 Capes found himself going backwards.

In Britain it had been too easy for too long. My heart was not in it. Every competition against British opposition was a bore. I knew I would win. How could anybody expect motivation when it was as straightforward as that? At least in other countries there were two or three men pushing each other. In Britain there was me all alone way out in front.

It must have been a bit like that for Allan Wells, Seb Coe and Steve Ovett during 1980, but at least that was an Olympic year when they had to be at their peak for their competition. For me, it had been that way year after year for six or seven years, and it is hard to find that little extra you need in major championships when you have been sitting on your bottom in domestic events all year.

I could win everything at home, putting between 19.50 and 20 metres. I have thrown that far from a standing position. The UK Championships in the first season after Montreal was a perfect illustration of this. I threw only 20.04 metres but I still beat Winch by more than a metre and the third guy by two metres. So you motor along in second gear and suddenly you are expected to go out in a major event against world champions and pop out a throw of 21 metres.

It is not possible. You have to build up to a big throw, and after Montreal there was no incentive to do that. Moscow was too far away to be a challenge, and 1977 was just another year.

I put on weight, I lost interest in the event, I became bored. I was surviving in easy competitions, going through the motions. I would train for as many hours as ever but I was not pushing myself. I would tell myself that I had done this or that, but I knew deep down that I was conning myself. I was not training hard. I was taking short cuts.

It began to happen in 1977. I was becoming a lazy sod. I was living in a dream world. I was drinking, having a good time, accepting invitations to dinners, parties and presentations, living off my reputation, happy to sit back. I was complacent. I even kidded myself that I was still one of the best, and sometimes I could do just enough to convince others. But I wasn't. Where I won I was winning with bad performances.

Just occasionally I could raise myself. I started the year brilliantly with 68 feet 8 inches at the Cosford Games, a UK all-comers best on a day when I was suffering from an inflamed muscle in my right shoulder. I also won the national indoor title and a couple of international indoor matches, and was never below 20.30 metres.

At the European Indoor Championships I was too shocked by the Icelander Halldorsson, who opened with a personal record, to do better than second with 20.46 metres, but it was the fourth successive year I had finished in the gold or silver medal place in the event.

Just to make amends for that, I beat him three times in

the space of a few days when he came to Britain in May, defeating the 1972 Olympic champion Komar for good measure in one of the same competitions, and making a useful start to the season with 20.98 metres at Southampton – the world's longest putt at that stage of the season. Then I beat American Paul Shmock and improved the year's world best to 20.99 just four days after another thrower had struck my heel with a shot in a warm-up throw. The moral, I guess, is: if you can't beat him, crock him. But even that didn't work.

Sounds good, doesn't it? Who said I wasn't still the best? I even found time to promote my own meeting at Spalding. The turn-out was fantastic: 8000 – as many as we could pack into the arena – came to see Brendan Foster, Sebastian Coe, Jane Colebrook, another local star who had won a European indoor title that year, and David Jenkins.

What a day that was! I was the hero of my own meeting. My throw of 21.30 metres, just $1\frac{1}{4}$ inches short of 70 feet, was my best of the season. What I wasn't to know was that it would remain my best for three years! Not until I came back a new man in Olympic year was I to come close to that distance again. That was the peak.

It was not my only contribution to the best afternoon's athletics ever seen in East Anglia. They let me out on the track later, and I beat Brendan Foster. It wasn't quite his usual distance – only 200 metres – but I reckoned the weight I was carrying, around 315 pounds at the time, evened things up nicely. Stuart Storey was announcing. That race gave him a lot of fun.

'In lane one, we have Brendan Foster,' he said 'In lanes two, three and four, Geoff Capes.'

But the joke was on Foster. I was so fast from the gun he never came close. I won in 24.9 seconds, with Big Bren six-tenths of a second behind me. It was all in a good cause, of course, and I must not forget to mention that Bren had been out for a 20 mile run that morning.

Nothing much went right from there. I lost to Stahl-berg by $2\frac{1}{2}$ feet in an international match up near the

Arctic Circle in Finland, scraped a win in the Europa Cup semi-finals at Crystal Palace with only 20.11 metres, and then beat Schmock and Feuerbach in a poor contest at Gateshead. And all I could manage in the European Cup final was fourth with 20.15 metres – 5 feet behind Beyer's winning putt.

In 1978, it was worse. I should have been up for a major year of Commonwealth and European Championships, but I wasn't. My best was 20.68 metres (67 feet 10¼ inches), and while it still ranked me in the world top ten it was not near what I should have been capable of producing. I won the Commonwealth title – the only other champion to defend successfully was Jamaican sprinter Don Quarrie – and I endured Prague. Fortunately, I have forgotten the rest!

In 1979 I slipped backwards for the fourth successive year. My best was 20.49 metres. For the first time in six years I was not in the world top ten. I was fifth in the Europa Cup final. I was not training. I had lost interest, and by 1979 I was overweight, too.

I felt like a Cyril Smith that year. I was pear-shaped. I was strong still, but what a terrible shape! I'd had fifteen years without a normal life, fifteen years when there was only one thing which mattered to me. Finally I'd become bored with it and rebelled against it. I was like a top actor turning to drink. I knew I was as good as anybody and I'd grown over-confident. I was believing that I could do it without training. I couldn't.

Fortunately, I still had friends and a family who believed in me. My wife, Stuart and many friends whose opinions I respected kept on at me. They hurt me. They tried hard to hurt me. I was called a fat slob, overweight, useless, anything to make me realize what had happened to me. I had rows with Gillian, rows with Stuart, all because they were trying to shake me out of my complacency. For a time I couldn't see it, refused to see it, but slowly it came home to me.

In the end, it was not so much the insults that made me change but the realization that I'd slipped so badly. I

108

became choked off with being fifteenth in the world and seeing dummies ahead of me who didn't deserve to be there. In August 1979, I talked things over with Stuart. He was straight with me. He would help but it had to be all the way. No half-measures this time. He agreed to give up a year of his time if I would commit myself totally to becoming the best again. I agreed. The comeback started that same month.

Curiously, I won the Thames Television strongest man programme at that time. I was out of condition, overweight and undertrained but I had enough strength to win that kind of event. That October I also beat the world record for lifting tyres. Actually, you don't exactly lift them. They put the tyres on you while you stand there. I had achieved a record of fifty-one in 1976, but that had been improved to sixty. This time I lifted seventy-three weighing $1058\frac{1}{2}$ pounds. It did not prove I was an athlete again, but it showed I was just as strong as I used to be.

But the training hurt. I ran, I bounded, I did mobility work. For a long time I did not even lift weights. I just kept telling myself that I was as good as anybody in the world but that it had taken me three years to build up the desire to prove it again. But, before I could do that, I had to get myself into serious shape again. I had to get 6 inches off my stomach and put those inches back on my chest and back.

Storey had not pulled any punches with Geoff. 'Fat slob' had been an expression he had used frequently to describe him in 1979, and the standards he demanded that autumn would have frightened off lesser men. 'Somewhere inside that flabby body was an athlete trying to get out,' he said. 'That was my role. To find that athlete again. It had always been Geoff's strength, his athleticism. He had never been a muscle-bound heavy. He had been fast, explosive, aggressive.

'Yes, I was nasty at times to him. I can be pretty cruel when I want to be, when I think it is necessary. And that year it was

necessary. I was determined, with his help, to make him look like a real athlete again and, all credit to him, once he had made the decision, he never faltered. He cursed and he swore on occasions but he never quit.'

There was one other factor driving Capes. The British Board had introduced an Elite Squad, an exclusive group of athletes who would be given special financial support and, more significantly, excused the anxiety of contesting the Olympic Trials. Capes was not among the group, not even when others such as 1500 metres runners Graham Williamson and John Robson were added later. The rejection hurt. The determination grew. It was the stimulus he had needed.

In early 1979 I would not have been able to run a lap of the Haringey track. Soon I would run a mile of it before every training session there. I was feeling myself again, and beginning to admire what I was seeing in the mirror again. I had also been having a few chats with a group of head shrinkers. Stuart had heard them give a lecture at Bisham Abbey during a seminar there. They were business associates of an American whose mind process was called the 'Inner Game'. It was based on the theory that, if you concentrate on one aspect of your performance completely, this will exclude all other thoughts that might interfere with the performance. I was a perfect guinea pig for that theory. I was always thinking of other things.

They came to see me at Haringey. They decided that I should concentrate everything on my right leg – the knee. It plays an important part in technique and, by thinking only of that, I was not worrying about my hips, my head, my shoulders and everything else down to my little toe. I was told to give my knee marks out of ten for its performance. That way my mind would not interfere with every other element of my throw.

Whether it worked or not, I could never tell. I went to New Zealand for the SPTV-Pan Am international track series with a group of Britons including Allan Wells,

Mike McLeod and Bill Hartley, and I certainly performed well. Maybe it was just the intensive training I
had been doing. Whatever it was, I climaxed the tour by
beating the 1979 world number two, Reijo Stahlberg,
and putting 20.76 metres (68 feet 1 inch) in Auckland,
my best for three years and good enough to have ranked
me fourth in the world the previous year.

I thought that would be good enough to get me added
to the Elite Squad. But I was told that there was not
another meeting for a month, and that nothing could be
done immediately. Yet, two days after the long flight
from New Zealand, I was competing for Britain again in
my last indoor international, against West Germany at
Cosford. There was no opposition as usual and I won
comfortably. I had decided already to miss the European
Indoor Championships, and so I went straight back to
the weights room and gym.

The season started for me on 3 May, and what a merry
month of May it was! I was superbly fit, enormously
strong, and very quick and aware again. All my old
enthusiasm was back. I was enjoying training and enjoying competition. I wanted to do well. I had waited three
years for this, and I wasn't going to waste a moment.

On that third day of May I went to Enfield to help my
club, Enfield, in the GRE British League Division Four.
It was not the most exalted of competitions, but it was a
suitably quiet event in which to find out how far I had
come. It was quite a way. In a chill wind, I opened with
20.13 metres, a 39 centimetre improvement on the five-
year-old league record, and had two more putts at 19.97
and 20.13 before I called it a day.

Two weeks later, I motored down to Cwmbran for
England's match against Wales, Hungary and the
Netherlands. There was nobody there to offer a challenge, but I felt right for something good. It was not long
coming. I putted 20.57, 20.85, 21.28, 20.91, 21.68, 21.46.
Every putt was better than anything else I did in 1979;
all but one were better than anything I had done since
1977. The fifth round putt was also a British, Common-

111

wealth and United Kingdom all-comers record – my first ever over 71 feet. It was 13 centimetres better than my own British and Commonwealth record, and it moved me to ninth on the world all-time list – just 1 centimetre ahead of Hartmut Briesenick. Only Beyer and the reinstated professional Oldfield putted further during 1980. Incredibly, the technique had gone by the sixth putt but I still managed 21.46.

Six days later I went to Belfast for an unheralded meeting. Brendan Foster and Steve Ovett came too, and it must have been the most unpublicized meet in the United Kingdom that summer. We slipped into that troubled place, and slipped out, and the newspapers in London barely recorded the fact. Yet I threw 21.50, my third best ever, and had a second best round of 21.14.

Next came a match for the Amateur Athletic Association against the West London Institute, which is better known in athletics as Borough Road College. Their circle is not ideal; it is close against a railing which separates the track from the busy Great West Road, with a grass verge behind it which almost touches your nose at the start of the throw.

That night things were made worse by appalling organization. For a reason I never established, they changed the time of the shot. I arrived more than 90 minutes before the time specified in my letter from the AAA to find the shot about to start. They refused to delay proceedings, so the competition started without me while I warmed up. I came in for the second round, still boiling with anger at their rudeness, and won easily with 20.91 metres.

Another AAA match at Loughborough was next on the schedule – the annual match against Loughborough Past and Present. I had always supported it, and always thoroughly enjoy it, but that cool June evening with its occasional shower turned out to be hot for me in more ways than one.

First the physiotherapist, while massaging my shoulders and neck – my regular treatment before competi-

112

tion – used the wrong ointment, a heat-producing embrocation. It was like having hot oil poured on to my back. I was on fire. My eyes watered; it was so hot. I began the competition with an ice pack strapped under my vest to sooth the pain.

But the heat did me no harm. My series was 21.13, 21.35, 21.31, 21.04: four consecutive 21 metre putts – something I had never achieved in my life.

By now, of course, I was a member of the Elite Squad. There was no need for me to compete in the Olympic Trials, and I had no intention of doing so, It was just about the only advantage I could see in being a member of that exclusive group. The only money I had been given that season in preparation for the Olympics had come from the Sports Aid Foundation, a grant which took Stuart and I to Spain for a week's training in April and paid our joint expenses for travelling to Haringey and Woolwich each week.

Curiously, the decision to add me to the squad had not been unanimous. At least one member of the Board had voted against me. No, it was not the officials one would expect. It was a fellow athlete, a vote cast against me by post by one of the athletes who represent us on the Board's council. With friends like that, who needs officials?

In the end, it did not make any difference to what happened in Moscow. The best system in the world, the most money, the best attention – none of them could have prevented the disaster that happened on the last Sunday in June. I was not throwing, I was not lifting, I was not even standing. I was lying in my own front room watching the television like most other family men on that day of the week. Unlike them, though, when I came to get up, I couldn't.

There was one consolation. I had made the effort. I could have continued to go through the motions as I had in 1979, trained half-heartedly and gone to Moscow for the ride. I am happy that I didn't. I could never have lived with myself not knowing for the rest of my life whether I might have won that gold had I tried.

113

14

Living a Lie

*Amateur athletics will continue to revise its rule on 'amateurism'
during the 1980s until the word ceases to have any vestige of its
original meaning. It would be better now to accept the* fait
accompli, *recognize that athletes are being paid illicitly and rid the
sport of the hypocrisy by following the example of tennis, cricket
and table tennis in abolishing the distinction between paid and
unpaid. Until that day, amateur athletics will continue to be, as
Herman David, chairman of the All-England Club, once said of
tennis, 'a living lie'.*

The Inland Revenue know precisely how much money I
earned as an amateur athlete. It was all in my income tax
returns, every last penny of my payments from the sport
and every penny which the sport cost me in expenses, all
legal and above board.

Well, not quite. By the law of the land, I am an honest
and law-abiding citizen. By the laws of my sport, I suffer
from what they regard as the most horrible crime –
ineligibility.

In athletics the word is all-important. Quite simply
the rule states that an athlete is ineligible to compete in
amateur athletics if he 'has, at any time, been financially
interested in any athletic meeting in which he was
entered'. That one sub-section of a rule ensures that just
about every athlete whose fame would fill a phone-box
with spectators is ineligible.

Of course, few are declared ineligible. Athletes who

are banned are usually those honest enough to admit they have received money for competing. Brian Oldfield, one of the shot putters I competed against often in 1980, was among the outstanding Americans banned for several years for honesty.

They only let him back when the International Amateur Athletic Federation came to realize that its own laws would not stand examination in a proper court of law. They could not afford to have the amateur rules tested in that way, so those banned were allowed back again.

Brian and others had the courage to become professional athletes openly in the United States. Most of us take what we loosely call 'expenses' on the amateur circuit in Europe. You only have to see the queues of athletes waiting outside an appointed hotel room after every invitation meeting on the Continent to know how many depend on 'expenses'. The word goes out that expenses will be paid in a certain room. Often you are still there in the early hours, waiting. It pays to be at the front. If the meeting has had a poor crowd, there may not be enough money to go round. That happened once to me in Italy.

The IAAF cannot prove that the expenses are above the pitiful standard they regard as acceptable. Even if they could, their case would be thrown out by a court of law. Their rule book is so full of holes that any lawyer worth his salt would run rings round it.

But, if they could prove a case for ineligibility, and if they could make it stick, most of the athletes of an international standard in Western Europe, Africa, America, Australia and New Zealand whose names are known to the general public would be banned.

It does not take Kojak to detect that the rules are being broken. Do the IAAF think that men with wives and children – some of whom bring those dependants on the circuit with them – and without full-time jobs can afford to spend three months of each summer travelling round Europe as amateur athletes?

115

Perhaps they do. Perhaps they believe we are living in an age when the best athletes are born with silver spoons in their mouths and live on allowances from papa. Perhaps. But they would be wrong.

I'll tell you how we do it – we make meeting promoters around the world pay a fair and honest rate for our services. The more famous we are, the more certain to pull in extra spectators and give them something to get excited about, the more we demand. We make them pay what the market will stand. We put a lot into our sport and we take our share in return. It is good, honest capitalism.

We are not going to get rich on it. For most of us, it does little more than recompense us for loss of earnings from full-time jobs and the heavy expenses of keeping ourselves competitive with the best in the world.

The system is well organized. There is a payments structure. The meeting promoters gather before the year begins, calculate which of them pays each part of the travelling expenses of those coming from outside Europe, and agree the highest fees they will pay. It would take an athlete with incredible pulling power to push the price higher.

The established athlete can name his own price within that structure, or at least negotiate. How much he will get depends on who he is, where he comes from, and in what event he competes. At one time, Americans were making money just because there was a lot of money around in America, and the promoters were saddled with a lot of bums.

Promoters are wise to it now, and the second-rate American looking for a cheap trip around Europe finds it tough going. One American sprinter with a well-known name was turned away from the best European meets in 1980 because his recent win record was so bad.

There are various other yardsticks for arriving at the final fee. In some events a world record will be worth extra, but a world record out of the blue is worth less than one which can be publicized in advance. That way it draws extra spectators. And a world record at an Olympic distance is worth more than one at 600 or 1000 metres.

The class of entry is important, too. Geoff Capes against nobody is worth little in public appeal. Geoff Capes against the best shot putters in the world, or a selection of them, is good pre-meet promotion. If one of the throwers then breaks a record and it makes extra media coverage, there is a bonus at the end of the day.

So an athlete agrees his 'expenses' and his bonuses – so much for an exciting high-level competition, a bit more for European or world records. The system does have its quirks. A group of athletes travelling together with a star among them can use him to gain entry and, even better, expenses for themselves.

A friend of mine went to a European meet, performed well and when he turned up for his expenses was asked who he was with. When he replied that he wasn't with anybody, he did not get a cent. But he saw someone he had beaten walk out with $400.

Track men obviously get more than those in field events. But, the better known you are, the more extrovert and controversial, the greater reaction you get from the crowd, the more you are worth to a promoter. Ilie Nastase may not have won much in tennis recently but he still pulls crowds.

The rows I have had, the punch-ups, the disqualification in Prague, have never done me any harm financially. I'm better known because of them. I'm willing to help promote a meeting, too, attend press conferences, do stunt pictures, and appear on television. I even stunted an arm-wrestling contest with Feuerbach to promote a meeting at Crystal Palace one year. Promoters like that. That's why men like John Walker and Don Quarrie are always welcome at meets. No only are they big names but they are happy to put themselves out to help.

That is one of the reasons I made demands when I was a major attraction. These demands made good publicity

117

for the meeting. Some were good for me, too. As I wrote earlier, I was responsible for a promoter having the circle at Crystal Palace moved from the backwoods into the front of the main stand. I wanted to be seen, to be noticed; I wanted the event to have a prime position.

Throwers get a raw deal except in the States and Scandinavia. We are makeweights in too many places, just there to fill out the programme. But we can give value for money as well as any other athletes. A shot competition given the limelight, with a good announcer, can be exciting stuff.

Throwers are the extroverts of athletics. We are like the forwards in rugby – big men who don't get star billing. We feel put upon. The runners, like the rugby half-backs, have the clean-cut image; we're the dirty brigade. Everybody is against us: the promoters who will not pay us like runners, and the federations who are not interested in developing our events.

So we band together. We're closer than any other groups in athletics. We work twice as hard for half as much and we put something back. Very few runners come back as coaches; but many throwers do. I have done, Winch has, Howard Payne has. So has John Hillier. We're more concerned for the future of our events than runners.

The first money I made from athletics was by courtesy of the British Amateur Athletic Board. They selected me for an international match in Paris against the French. Usually, the most you could come away with from any dual meet was a medallion. The French that day handed our Napoleonic gold coins.

They were worth a bit, as we soon discovered. There was a Frenchman there offering to buy them from us. How many you were awarded depended on your result. The winners had four. The buyer was paying £60 each. In 1971, that was far above the £100 maximum allowed for prizes.

Airline tickets are the usual currency for paying athletes. Say you are going to a meet in Norway, and then

118

on to a meet in Sweden. You will receive two return tickets from London, one to each venue. One, of course, you can cash. The two promoters then split the cost of your services between them.

But there is plenty of cash, too. Team managers know about this but accept it. Money makes the amateur athletic world go round. The managers just make themselves scarce when the expenses are paid.

The most I have picked up from one meeting is about $1,250. More common is $400 to $500. A star middle-distance runner, a world-record holder or an Olympic champion who is a major drawing card may get $5000 or more. But there are few meets which can afford that sort of money, even for the exceptional athlete.

It is a crazy situation – national federations everywhere are broke or pleading poverty and existing off government handouts and commercial sponsors, while the best promoters know the way to make big profits.

I have been on both sides of the fence – poacher turned gamekeeper. I have described earlier how I organized my own meeting at Spalding in 1977, the Dewhurst Games. And it made a profit shared by my first club, Holbeach, and the local Round Table.

Everybody is welcome to look at the books of that meeting. We paid the athletes their proper expenses. We were not tight like national federations. They received what Geoff Capes thought were reasonable expenses for the time they had invested and the trouble to which they had gone. There was none of the British Board's 3p or 4p a mile for petrol and second-class rail fares. My stars were expected to travel like stars, and eat like I do.

Our intention was to encourage an interest in athletics in a place unaccustomed to major sports events. So we charged only 50p entrance and the stadium was full to its capacity of 8000. Thanks to Dewhurst's sponsorship, every penny at the gate was profit, and we netted more than £4000 for charity. Imagine then the profit from a crowd of 17,000 at Crystal Palace where top priced tickets are £4.

119

The International Federation, the British Board and the national associations have made token attempts to enforce their rules but they recognize, I believe, the facts of life. As I retire, they are talking of a change in their rules. It will not change anything – just make legal what happens now 'illegally'.

Twice I have come under investigation for accepting illegal payments. The first was at the Glenlivet Games at Edinburgh in 1977 in what became known as the 'Meadowbank affair'.

That time I had to make a full and detailed report of all I had received and how I had spent every penny of it – the trains or the cars, the hotels, the meals, everything. That was no problem. I could account for every last farthing.

They knew, of course, that the next day I had competed in another part of Scotland at Coatbridge. Naturally I received expenses all over again. But did I charge those expenses from home again? That is what the Scottish AAA would love to know. Fortunately, the local council who had invited us to their meeting refused to reveal to the SAAA any details of expenses claimed. Quite rightly, they decided that we had supported their meeting and it would have been unsporting to tell tales on their guests.

That decision may have saved some of Britain's 1980 Olympic team from suspension. Even now, I am not going to reveal what Coatbridge have so jealously guarded because many involved are still competing as amateurs.

The second case was at Gateshead, where the promoter was again the local council. They paid me £250 to compete. I even signed for the money when they gave it to me. None of those Donald Duck or Jimmy Carter signatures which appear on athletes' expenses. I signed my own name.

Daring? Not a bit of it. I knew that the old guard were hotting up their investigations of shamateurism and I had covered myself in advance. I had even written to the

Southern Counties AAA, my area governing body, informing them of the payment.

I told them that the costs of organizing their Southern shot squad, phone bills, stationery and such like for that year would be £200. Rather than charge them directly I would take it out of my Gateshead expenses. The remaining £50 were legitimate expenses for getting to Gateshead.

They agreed to that idea, and the investigation into Gateshead's payments has never worried me greatly. I made a statement, as did all those competing there, and I feel I am in the clear.

Outside athletics, of course, I have made a bob or two from competing. If the profit from an event is for charity or fund-raising for sport, I'll be there for nothing. But, if it is to line somebody's pocket, I want my share. I was just careful.

Sometimes it backfires. When I won the strongest man competition for Thames Television, my winnings should have been more than £1000. I reckoned that half for me and half for Holbeach Athletic Club would be fair – something for the sport, something for my efforts.

But I was on police leave at the time. When I won, it was suggested that the Police Benevolent Fund could do with a donation. How could I refuse? So that turned out to be a charity appearance!

I still came out of the event ahead of the game. The glasswear they gave me for winning must have been worth £600. I wasn't complaining.

Amateurism in athletics is dead. It has been a ghost of its original self for years. Thousands still compete for fun. That's great. But there comes a time when you begin to devote more and more time to the sport, helping it, earning it money, promoting and projecting it. Then you deserve payment.

During my career I have received money from the Winston Churchill Foundation, from the Sports Aid Foundation, and from sponsors such as Dewhurst in the form of free meat and provisions. Some were called

121

scholarships, others élite grants. But always they were given to me because I was good at athletics. They were payments to an amateur.

They were legal because our governing body decided they were legal. To you and me the money would not appear any different from generous expenses from athletics meetings. If one lot of money made me a professional, why not the other? That is the hypocrisy of the amateur rule.

If being a good athlete improves your standard of living, ensures that you eat better, drive a better car and enjoy training trips abroad at somebody else's expense, you are a professional. Every Russian athlete of world class is a professional. So is every American, Finn, West German and French athlete. So are the Britons.

It is time the sport recognized that, and allowed everybody to enjoy the fruits of our talents as athletes. Then we could all get back to enjoying athletics.

Would I compete again as a shot putter if the sport was made open? Not now. It is too late. The sport has become too serious at the highest level. The fun has gone out of it. I get more fun now out of Highland Games and strongest men contests.

For those I leave behind and for future generations, it is time the sport acknowledged that the best athletes are paid and deserve to be paid. It is time they were allowed to be paid.

15

The Coach and Coaching

Stuart Storey on Geoff Capes

'For me, Geoff was just a lad who had problems with whom I developed a relationship and who, in the end, became a bloody good mate. Never make the mistake of thinking that Geoff Capes was created, by me or anybody else. Geoff was born to be a great shot putter.

To start with I had only a basic AAA coaching qualification in shot putting. I was a student at Loughborough. Geoff and I taught each other the event as we went along, watching a lot of films, talking to many people, and wherever I went in the world as an international hurdler I kept a positive eye on the shot.

Then we would go on to the chunk of concrete we called a circle at Carter's Park, move the plough that was always parked on it and try out what we'd learnt. This was a good circle psychologically – it was downhill!

Lots of people helped. When Geoff moved to Peterborough and I went south, Les Mitchell took over for a time, just keeping an eye on him. Wilf Paish helped a lot, Tommy Clay did his bit, so did Geoff's mates in the club, so did many I can't even remember now. Okay, to start with, I was the only one who could tell him what to do and that was an important part of his development. But technically he could have been coached by quite a few people. Let's be honest, if Geoff had been left to his own devices, untouched by coaches, he would still have thrown a long, long way.

Coaches have to accept that there are athletes who are champions, who have that greatness about them. They cannot create that. Capes had the sort of ability that meant he would have been great whoever had taken told of him.

Too often, when a coach is lucky enough to come together with a

123

man like that, people immediately assume he is a good coach. They think of his success in purely technical terms, that what the athlete has done makes that man a good coach. Yet, for the very reason that he is working with greatness, it may be that he does not need to be a good coach in the technical sense.

Obviously, if the relationship lasts and prospers, there must be something of value there. But my coaching was human as much as technical. We learnt the techniques together, and shot putting became a special interest of mine – the analysis, the bio-mechanics and the psychology. That rubbed off on Geoff and he became interested in coaching; we tried out things together and success was a combined effort.

But Geoff always had what it takes. He was enormously strong and had more fast fibres in his muscles than any big man I know. And was he aggressive! In those early days he was all aggression. He finally mellowed into a nice guy. Sometimes I wish he hadn't. Nice guys begin to accept defeat.'

Geoff Capes on Stuart Storey

Stuart Storey has been a mother and father to me. When I've had problems, he's heard them first, and it's been like that since I was thirteen. I spoke to my mother and I respected her but I never felt I could go to her. My father is a nice guy, the salt of the earth type, a guy you'd like to have a pint with. But Stuart was my shoulder, something always there to lean on.

He wasn't that much older than I – less than seven years. I had a British junior international vest before he had competed in the Olympic Games in Mexico. But he was a man from my own village who had done what I wanted to do. He had been through it and done it, and there was no other person in that village who could have been for me what Stuart was.

We grew up in the event together. We had our successes and our failures together. He taught me the game – not the pure technique only but how to compete, how to keep stable in competition, what to eat, how to warm up, all the little things that a purely theoretical coach with only paper qualifications cannot possibly hope to know. Stuart knew because he had been there himself.

'Coach' is an odd word. With Stuart and I it's not the right word. He is a motivator, a helper, an inspiration. He's more than a coach. I learnt from him, from his experiences, just as most kids learn from their folks.

Even today he helps me, perhaps with the right words or the right approach to a problem. We're not always friends. I hate him sometimes. He can be spiteful. 'If it wasn't for me, you'd be nowhere,' he's said before now. And I can be hurtful back. 'But for your connection with me, you'd never have got a job in television,' I've told him.

I got to him so deeply one evening before the Moscow Games that he hung up on me. I loved my triumph that night. We apologized to each other next day but I felt I'd out-talked the talker.

We're just like father and son; we fall out and we drift apart but we come back together because really I think we both have a lot of time for each other.

He knows my weaknesses: complacency, lethargy, taking too much account of others and not concentrating on what I am capable of myself, and an occasional lack of self-confidence. He knows I can be upset, put off, interfered with by all about me – the family, the job, what people might say and think. In that sense, too, he has been a protector.

As a coach? Not bad at all. He knows when to prod me and how best to do it. And he has given up a lot of time to do it properly. I'll always be grateful for that.

My year used to begin at the end of September. I might have rested for a couple of weeks at the end of the previous season but then I took time to get myself fit to train. That was important. You cannot go lifting enormous weights when you are unfit. You have to be fit first.

It is a funny sight seeing a man of 23 stone running, but I used to do 3 mile runs for a month before I began my weights programme. I was more like a gymnast than a

125

thrower. I would run, do sit-ups and gym work, climb ropes and exercise on the wall bars.

By the beginning of November I would be ready for the weight-training programme, but the gym work would continue alongside it. In 1976 I played basketball and volleyball to keep myself fit, and did plenty of jogging and sprinting.

The weight programme would be worked out after long talks with Stuart. We would sit down each autumn, work out how I felt, what I needed most, and where it would be possible for us to meet and when. Most years it would be twice each week, at Woolwich or Dartford, where he worked, or midway between the two of us at Enfield or Haringey.

The year before Moscow, we met on Thursdays and Fridays, and I would stay overnight at his home. In the two to three hour sessions on those two days we would do the heavy-weight work because for this I needed assistance. For the rest of the week I would do the same exercises but with less weight.

In those two weekly sessions, often in the weights room at the superbly equipped New River sports centre at Haringey, I would lift about 150 tons in a session. We would work out a schedule of sets and repetitions in each of the lifts I did.

My lifts were bench, squat, deadlift, power clean, clean and jerk, seated military press, seated neck press, dumb-bell incline seated, step-ups and sit-ups.

We would calculate a system of doing eight sets of ten at a certain weight in each lift. Nearer the competition we would cut down on sets and reps but the weights would be the same. It was the pyramid system of bench pressing – say, 120 pounds ten times and then gradually increasing the weight and reducing the number to a single lift of 500 pounds.

When I really decided to make a last go of it in 1980, when Stuart snapped me out of my complacency of the previous years, he had to make me athletic again. One method was the sit-up. I had developed an enormous

126

gut, and that had to go.

But the sit-up is a mean thing for a big man. My weight is largely in my shoulders and arms and upper body. I have short legs – 32 inch inside leg, which is incredibly short for a man of 6 feet 5 inches. So sit-ups are difficult for me. For one thing I had to anchor my toes under a wall bar.

Stuart started me off on just ten, and they were pure agony. Then we worked our way up to two sets of fifteen. Finally, I could do seventy-five straight off, maybe as many as 150 in a single training session. That is why I looked as if I had lost weight in 1980. I had in fact simply re-distributed my weight, put it back in the right places. My gut had gone.

I trained hard, five days a week, one day easy and rested on the seventh. I would also be coaching every weekend and several nights each week. I would also be in touch with those I coached but who lived too far away to come to my sessions; I worked out there training programmes and took calls from fathers who wanted help with their little Billys. I would be living and breathing track and field sixteen hours each day.

So what did I teach them? Perhaps it would be best to give here a typical lesson I would give to the novice. It is a progressive lesson, so don't expect to master it in one attempt. It will take time to practise the early sections before you progress to the full technique.

The grip is the first element to learn. With palm uppermost, place the shot on the base of the fingers of the right hand gently spread. All four fingers should be fairly close together, depending to a degree on the shot, hand and finger sizes. The thumb should be close to the index finger so that it is not only supporting the shot from below but able to participate in the final push at release.

The carry position is the shot cradled against the neck and under the jaw. The throwing arm should be in a natural position with the elbow, neither too high nor too low.

Now the power position. Stand with your legs astride,

about $2\frac{1}{2}$ to 3 feet (75 to 90 centimetres) apart, placing the weight on the right leg and with your knees bent. Now turn your shoulders a quarter right (90 degrees) without allowing your hips and legs to move out of their position. Bend slightly forward.

Imagine a javelin thrust through your hips in this position. It should point in the throwing direction. A second javelin thrust through your shoulders would be at 90 degrees to the hip javelin. That puts your back in the direction of the throw.

Now put your left arm across your stomach or, if it feels easier, hold it out straight in front of you in the opposite direction from that you will be throwing in. Raise your throwing arm into position, holding the shot in your hand at your neck. If another javelin pierced your right foot from heel to toe, it would be parallel with the shoulder javelin.

Now you are in the best position for utilizing all the latent forces available, assuming your hips are under you – that is as long as you are not sticking your bottom out. You have to learn how to jump into this position. So stand with feet parallel and fairly close, facing in the opposite direction from the throw. Suddenly twist your legs and hips, and jump into the power position. Make sure you keep your shoulders as they were before the jump and that you twist your right foot 90 degrees left by the time it lands. Keep looking forward during and after your jump (180 degrees from the throw direction). Practise this jumping until you hit the proper power position perfectly every time, Now try it with the shot at your neck.

Next comes the mini-glide. Stand as you were before you jumped into the power position. Bend your knees as if to sit down ('sit') and bend forward from the waist. Extend your left leg backwards keeping it slightly above the ground in the air ('reach'). Now make a little jump on the right leg and, twisting your right foot, leg and hips 90 degrees left, land in the power position ('twist').

Try this without the shot and then with the shot. In

twisting and jumping keep looking ahead of you and get your hips under you. On arrival in the power position, your weight should be largely on your right leg, and your shot and your right foot should be in a plumb line with each other. Look at one point in the background ahead of you throughout the movement.

Now the standing throw. You are in the power position looking 180 degrees from the throw direction and keeping your shoulders from unwinding. Rock forward, pushing yourself from right foot to left foot, at the same time sweeping leftward with your left arm to 'separate' your shoulders. As you rock, your whole body moves into the throwing direction and your right knee tilts inward, placing the shin of your right leg into a forward-slanting angle. At the same time, bend your left leg a little more.

Now lift your front knee and unwind your shoulders. As your left arm braces at your side, strike with the right arm. The quick lifting of the shot by the back and by the explosive straightening of the left leg coincides with the pulling down to the side of the left arm and the final unwinding of the shoulders and the striking of the right arm.

You should stay with the standing putt for a long time before trying the mini-glide putt in slow motion. It's like a slow-motion film of the technique, with you checking your position at each stage. At the 'sit', check that you are sinking deep enough, that the body is sufficiently bent in the hips and that the shot is outside the perpendicular plane of the rear edge of the circle. At the 'reach', ensure that the left leg is extended, unrotated and hovering above the ground. At the 'twist', pause to check on desired position. Are you still looking back? Are your shoulders square? Have you turned your right foot 90 degrees? Are your hips under you? If so 'throw'.

This last phase can be done in two distinct steps: (1) rock and sweep; and (2) lift and strike. Now you have perfected the mini-glide putt, you have perfected the full shot-putting action but with a short glide. Gradually you should shorten the pauses and finally do it non-stop.

Now you can try the half-glide putt. The action is the same as in the mini-glide but now you start extending your left leg, falling a little with your seat towards the centre of the circle. This will cause you to gain ground backwards, moving your body and the shot from the rear end of the circle towards the front. Don't cover more than about a foot (30 centimetres).

In the fall, make sure the upper body stays back, directly over the right foot. Again try it with pauses before you do it non-stop.

Finally we can try the full-glide putt. Falling on a little more will result in a full glide, which means that at the end of your glide your right foot will have travelled from the rear of the circle to the centre. You may pause after the 'sit' but at this stage do not pause after hitting the power position.

During the non-stop action the left arm should remain in its original position (at least 180 degrees from the throwing direction) and should start its 'sweep' only as the left leg hits the ground.

The torque (hips 'leading' the shoulders by nearly 90 degrees when hitting the power position) is vital before the actual putt action starts. If the left arm starts its sweep too soon, the torque will be lost. Practise it in front of a mirror.

Most important of all, don't expect too much too quickly. A runner may be able to go out and run, but a thrower cannot just go out and putt a shot. You have to serve your apprenticeship. It will take time, years probably, and however strong you are you will not throw to your full potential unless the action is right. Komar won the Olympic shot gold metal in 1972 in his mid-thirties. You have plenty of time. Be patient.

16

The Young Generation

Allan Wells, Olympic 100 metres champion in 1980, spoke for many in the British team at the end of 1980 when he said, 'There isn't a man in the British team more respected by the other athletes than Geoff Capes. People think of him as a rebel but he's been a great ambassador for the British team and no athlete has done more to help other members of the team. He'll be difficult to replace.'

Sebastian Coe had another idea. 'He'd make a great team manager. He commands enormous respect from the athletes, and he has shown many times that he is happy to stand up for them. I can't think of a better man for the job.'

He will not get the job, of course. Capes stood up once or twice too often for official liking. But his commitment to the sport is still far from finished.

The future for me is already assured. I had signed a professional contract to compete in the World's Strongest Man contest in America even before my last international match as an amateur athlete. In fact, the truth is that I competed in that event three weeks before my final appearance for Britain in the match against Sweden. This did not break the amateur rules because the programme was not scheduled to be screened on British television until long after the Sweden match.

Athletics was not fun for me any more. It all seemed too serious. Running 100 feet with a 400 pound fridge on your back may not be an Olympic event, but it is a good laugh. So is tossing the caber, lifting tyres, throwing a weight for height, and lifting bricks. They are fun sports, and I'll be happy doing them.

I have signed a three-year contract with the distributors of Reebok sports equipment in Britain and, soon after my last amateur appearances as an athlete, I opened a health studio a few miles from my home town in Spalding, in partnership with Tony Slaney, brother of international discus thrower Richard. These occupations will keep me busy, and there will be the Highland professional circuit and the strongest man event to put the jam on the bread and butter.

But athletics will not get rid of me completely. I want a part of the great future there could be for British throwing. Yes, a greater future than anything that has gone before. Not in 1981, because all athletics slump a little after an Olympic year, and in Britain the throws will slump that little bit more than usual without me. But in four and eight years' time Britain will have a fine generation of throwers.

There are lots of good kids now. George Brocklebank is one. He put aside his athletics when he was still at school because of his family's strongly held religious beliefs. I had to ask a friend of mine, an officer in the police force, to write to him explaining why the fulfilment of a God-given talent was so important. George has the talent to be outstanding.

Tony Zaidman, who broke the United Kingdom junior shot record last year with 17.42 metres, is another and there could be a real sensation coming along in the Cardiff boy, Chris Ellis. He beat the English Schools Championships junior boys' shot record by an unbelievable margin of more than 5 feet in 1980 – and he is only fourteen.

There is talent, but where is the expertise? Britain has national coaches, but there is not one professional specializing in shot to whom I would bother to send a kid for advice. The only two I would consider are Winch and myself, and that must be a snub to the expensive national coaching system we have in Britain.

132

Mind you, there must be something wrong with a coaching system when Britain is beaten at every Games by a nation as small as East Germany. The reason is not entirely political. Political objectives give athletes the will, but the way is open to every country. We must coordinate our sporting system better. We must improve our system for nurturing talent. What is to stop our finding a way that suits Britain? It may not be the East German way, but there has to be a better way because what we have at present simply does not work.

We need selection, not random chance. We need people going into the schools, offering advice, searching out specialist talent. There is far too much chance involved now. Too much potential is missed for ever because nobody is seeking it out.

Even in a Western democracy like the United States they have a system of seeking talent – the recruitment services of the universities. In America the athletics system breaks down in post-university days, when the athletes find themselves without the superb campus facilities and coaching, and they lose heart.

In Britain we have a well-organized club system. We have improving facilities. The Haringey club is a good example, a strong club built round impressive facilities. Where we fail is in the late-school and immediate post-school phase.

Athletics is an individual sport but it flourishes best in collectives, just like the one I enjoyed for a few weeks in San José. Training is so much more enjoyable when there is company, and so much more successful. A group of athletes who exchange ideas and knowledge keep improving, and so does their event.

That method of training is in many senses what I have tried to establish, and what Mike Winch had established independently. We have given up hoping that the governing body of our sport will produce a system, and we have made our own. It is makeshift. It depends still to some extent on luck, on promising kids finding us. But at least now Winch and I are two well-known, easily found,

133

specialists who are happy to be contacted. No father, schoolteacher or youth leader need look further.

Mike and I started the Southern Shot Squad together but had an argument over how things should be developed – but that's not a bad thing. Now we have two independent groups, both highly knowledgeable and each catering for different types – Mike for the smaller thrower, me for the big men. I will take any type of thrower. I help Susan Flack and Vanessa Vanterpool, outstanding junior international javelin throwers, and Timmy Isaacs, a discus thrower. It is not right that they do not have specialist coaches in their own events, but at least they have someone to turn to for advice. They can talk to me. Unfortunately, we are not together all the time, though my group visit me regularly, kipping on the lounge floor or in the bath, or occasionally dispossessing one of my children of a bed.

I am saving them from the scrap heap. Without advice they would lose interest. The father of a twelve-year-old from Luton phoned me, pleading for my help. His son was big and keen but nobody could help him. I listened, I made suggestions, I worked out a training programme. It is not perfect but it is a start. If only we had the money, we could make sure none of the promising kids is lost to the sport.

Throwing makes many more demands on a system than running, more demands on coaching and facilities, and throwers need a lot of encouragement. Runners will come through in their teens. Steve Ovett was a European silver medallist at eighteen. No thrower in the world has achieved that much so young. Beyer was exceptional when he won the Olympic shot title at twenty-one. Throwers have to develop a technique and it can only be built up over years.

They will need a long time to perfect those skills. They will not make it in a couple of years. They have to finish their growth-pattern first, develop their body. The average age for a throws champion is twenty-five or twenty-six. Some runners have retired by that age.

It's a long apprenticeship for a thrower. That is one of the reasons why so few want to take it up. Kids want immediate success. They know that sprinters can get into the British team in their teens. In the women's team almost all events have teenagers. So they go for the easy route to the top. They won't serve their time. Everybody wants to be a champion without being a challenger.

I have kids who come to me for coaching who think that because I am Geoff Capes they will get success immediately, that I can guarantee it by waving a magic wand. They cannot believe that it might take years. They probably would not believe that I do not have a single paper coaching qualification to my name.

All I can guarantee is to be there to put them on the right road, just as Stuart did for me all those years ago. Somewhere in Britain there is another lad, a special animal, big, strong and yet quick, explosive and aggressive. He might not be much good at school work, and he might even be a bit of a tearaway. But he has a special talent which this country needs and which properly nurtured might one day produce for it another champion. I would be delighted to help.

Meanwhile my new bible will be the *Guinness Book of Records,* not those of the IAAF and the British Board. I have to improve on hurling a 5 pound building brick 146 feet 1 inch, or lifting seventeen of them off a bench in a horizontal line. Then there is that record for lifting seventy-seven car tyres that I could strive to beat. It won't ever make up for that Olympic gold medal I never won but it will be a challenge. And that's what I enjoy.

Appendix 1

Geoff Capes's Progression

Date	Where held	Length of throw in metres
14.5.66	—	14.64
6.8.66	Holbeach	14.74
17.12.66	Cosford	14.91i
25.2.67	Stanmore	14.97i
8.4.67	Lincoln	15.30
10.6.67	Loughborough	15.87
29.7.67	Portsmouth	15.91
28.8.67	White City	15.97
16.9.67	Solihull	16.10
25.4.68	Cambridge	16.47
30.7.68	Holbeach	16.80
16.11.68	Cosford	17.26
3.5.69	Peterborough	16.89
26.5.69	White City	16.95
5.6.69	Loughborough	17.24
7.6.69	Grangemouth	17.47
8.8.70	White City	17.53
31.8.70	White City	17.73
30.1.71	Cosford	18.07i
27.2.71	Cosford	18.19i
24.4.71	Cambridge	17.91
1.5.71	Shotley Gate	18.33
3.6.71	Loughborough	18.35
12.6.71	Edinburgh	18.70
27.6.71	Paris	19.03
31.7.71	Holbeach	19.07
21.8.71	Edinburgh	19.48
26.4.72	Newham	19.56

26.7.72	Helsinki	20.18
14.7.73	Crystal Palace	20.27
19.7.73	Athens	20.34
31.7.73	East Berlin	20.47
6.1.74	Crystal Palace	20.59
19.1.74	Timaru	20.64
2.2.74	Christchurch	20.74
23.2.74	Madrid	20.82i
10.3.74	Gothenburg	20.95i
22.5.74	Crystal Palace	20.81
26.5.74	Crystal Palace	20.90
19.6.74	Crystal Palace	21.00
10.8.74	Crystal Palace	21.37
28.5.76	Gateshead	21.55
18.5.80	Cwmbran	21.68

i = indoors

Geoff set seventeen British records – the last fourteen shown in the above table (from Newham in 1972), one other at Newham that same day and two others at Helsinki on 26 July 1972 in the same competition. Seventeen records equals the most by a British athlete in one event.

On the day of his last competition, Britain versus Sweden, on 12 September 1980, he also still held the Commonwealth, United Kingdom All-Comers and the AAA National records.

Appendix 2

Internationals

Full GB Internationals — complete record

Year	Country/Competition	Place	Length (metres)
1969	Czechoslovakia	4	17.06
	France	6	16.43
1970	GDR	4	16.60
	Poland	3	17.72
1971	GDR (indoors)	3	17.11
	France (indoors)	2	18.19
	European Indoor Championships	10	17.84
	France	2	18.94
	European Championships	16	18.54
	West Germany	1	19.45
1972	Spain (indoors)	1	19.26
	European Indoor Championships	8	18.67
	Poland	2	19.51
	Finland, Spain	1	20.18
	OLYMPICS	20	18.94
	France	2	18.99
1973	GDR (indoors)	2	19.86
	Spain (indoors)	1	20.04
	European Indoor Championships	7	19.26
	GDR	2	19.92
	Greece, Belgium	1	20.34
	European Cup semi-final	1	20.15
	Hungary	1	19.90
	European Cup final	3	19.80
	Sweden	1	20.14

1974	Spain (indoors)	1	20.82
	European Indoor Championships	1	20.95
	GDR	1	21.00
	Poland, Canada	1	20.58
	Czechoslovakia	1	20.77
	European Championships	3	20.21
1975	Belgium (indoors)	1	20.46
	France (indoors)	1	19.87
	Spain (indoors)	1	19.93
	European Indoor Championships	2	19.98
	GDR	3	20.69
	European Cup semi-final	1	20.35
	European Cup final	1	20.75
	USSR	2	20.07
	Sweden	1	20.01
1976	European Indoor Championships	1	20.64
	USSR	2	21.15
	Poland, Canada	1	20.83
	OLYMPICS	6	20.36
1977	Italy (indoors)	1	20.30
	Spain (indoors)	1	20.62
	France (indoors)	1	20.69
	European Indoor Championships	2	20.46
	Finland	2	20.42
	European Cup semi-final	1	20.11
	European Cup final	4	20.15
	USSR	1	20.02
	West Germany	1	20.49
1978	West Germany (indoors)	1	19.89
	Spain (indoors)	1	19.77
	European Indoor Championships	3	20.11
	GDR	1	19.94
	European Championships	DQ	20.08
	Finland	1	20.68
1979	European Indoor Championships	2	20.23
	GDR (indoors)	1	20.01
	European Cup semi-final	1	19.70
	European Cup final	5	19.75
	Russian SFSR	2	19.60
1980	West Germany (indoors)	1	19.91
	OLYMPICS	5	20.50
	Sweden	1	19.39

His total of internationals – sixty-seven – is a record by a British athlete. Next best: Mike Bull – 66; Brenda Bedford – 65; Howard Payne – 61.

His total number of event wins in international matches – thirty-four – is also a record. Next best: Mary Rand – 29; Lyn Davies – 27 (excluding relays).

GB Junior Internationals:

1967	France	1	15.91
	Sweden	2	15.53
1968	West Germany	1	16.18
	(Discus)	4	42.02

England Internationals
(not including matches v. Scotland, Wales, N. Ireland)

1970	Commonwealth Games	4	17.06
1974	Commonwealth Games	1	20.74
1978	Commonwealth Games	1	19.77
1979	Canada	1	19.99
	Scotland, Norway, Belgium	1	20.40
1980	Wales, Holland, Hungary	1	21.68

For Europe

1978	v. USA	2	20.01
			(indoors)

Appendix 3

National Championships

AAA Championships

Year	Indoors Place	Indoors Length (metres)	Outdoors Place	Outdoors Length (metres)
1968		—	7	15.19
1969	2	16.48	7	15.45
1970		—	3	17.53
1971	1	18.07	2	18.30
1972	1	18.65	1	19.47
1973		—	1	20.27
1974	1	20.28	2	20.77
1975	1	19.92	1	20.20
1976		—	1	20.92
1977	1	20.63	1	20.70
1978	1	20.72	1	19.94
1979		—	1	19.39
1980		—	2	20.10

AAA Junior Championships
(12 pound shot)

Year	Place	Length (metres)
1966	1	17.14
1967	1	18.15

UK Championships

1977	1	20.04
1978	1	19.80
1979	1	19.00
1980		—

Capes's defeat in the 1970 AAA Championships by Jeff Teale (second with 18.02 metres) on 8 August at the White City was his last ever by a British athlete at the shot.

Best Performances – Competitions over 21 metres:

Date	Where held	Length (metres)
18.5.80	Cwmbran	21.68
28.5.76	Gateshead	21.55
24.5.80	Belfast	21.50
10.8.74	Crystal Palace	21.37
19.6.76	Crystal Palace	21.36
5.6.80	Loughborough	21.35
3.7.77	Spalding	21.30
22.8.76	Gateshead	21.20
8.5.76	Grangemouth	21.18
23.5.76	Kiev, USSR	21.15
18.6.80	Hull	21.12
12.6.76	Crystal Palace	21.04
14.7.76	Gateshead	21.03
26.5.80	Birmingham	21.03
19.6.74	Crystal Palace	21.00
9.5.76	Coatbridge	21.00
21.8.76	Rothesay	21.00